SAINT
BADASS

How Love Wins
The Power of Mindful Kindess

Be kind. It sounds simple, so why is it so difficult? Most of us recognize that being kinder and more present would not only improve our own lives and the lives of our loved ones, but also strengthen our communities and even our world. In fact, numerous scientific studies have confirmed that both living mindfully and being kind to others offer a host of benefits—from stronger relationships to longer life. Yet even if we truly care and are motivated to change, we find that old habits keep us coming back to the same self-centered cycle. With his book *How Love Wins,* Buddhist and educator Doug Carnine offers another path. In this simple but powerful guide, Carnine leads the reader through a 12-step process of transformation, opening a toolbox of skills and techniques that anyone can use to live more fully in the moment and be more kind to themselves and others. A lay Buddhist minister who has worked with hospice patients and prisoners, Carnine reassures us that everyone is capable of building a mindfully kind life—and making it stick.

Doug's book makes a critical contribution to evolving societies that nurture the well-being of every person. Ultimately, a nurturing society will be one where every person is committed to caring acts in their relationships with everyone they encounter. How Love Wins is a foundation for creating such a society. With warmth, compassion, and clarity it will guide you to a way of living that benefits you, at the same time it enriches the lives of everyone you encounter.

—Tony Biglan, author of *The Nurture Effect*

Kindness is the soil our loving relationships require for survival and growth. But can we learn to be kind, even if our past has been cruel? In this book, Carnine uses science, hands-on exercises, and real-life experiences from max-security prisoners to say yes—with great benefits for our happiness, fulfillment, and relationships. His mindful kindness practice is transformational, no matter how much pain is in your past. This powerful book takes any of us from a life of "me" to "we," from isolation to connection and love. In a world where kindness is so needed yet so little understood, How Love Wins is a must-read.

—Duana Welch, author of *Love Factually: 10 Proven Steps fromI Wish to I Do*

SAINT
BADASS

PERSONAL TRANSCENDENCE
IN TUCKER MAX HELL

DOUG CARNINE
with
Roy Tester, John Bruno, Cody Griffin,
and Roger "Tad" Price, Jr.

Saint Badass
Personal Transcendence in Tucker Max Hell

Doug Carnine

© 2017 Doug Carnine

First Edition

ISBN: 978-0-998-05090-4

Library of Congress Control Number: 2017910638

We must never forget that we may also find meaning in life even when confronted with a hopeless situation, when facing a fate that cannot be changed. For what then matters is to bear witness to the uniquely human potential at its best, which is to transform a personal tragedy into a triumph, to turn one's predicament into a human achievement.

—Viktor E. Frankl, *Man's Search for Meaning*

CONTENTS

ACKNOWLEDGMENTS

Without the help of these individuals, this book would not exist. Jerry Silbert, a colleague and good friend, has helped me extensively with many versions of the book. Barbara Gates gave me the encouragement and direction that moved me forward and kept me going. Caroline Pincus revamped the organization and clarified several sections. Geri Larkin was the "big idea" source for the book's title, provided initial input on what would stay and what would go, and helped recruit Ilima. Editor Ilima Loomis improved both the organization and the page-by-page readability of the book. The front cover art is by Roger "Tad" Price, who is also one of the principal contributors to the book. The cover was designed by Keirsten Lindholm, whose graphic talents are also showcased on the companion website, feedkindness.com. The book's design comes from Lynda Gansel. My thanks to Ashly Cupit who handled the book's production. Mauricio Valadrian created the video about the book, and Julie Hutchings helped develop the feedkindness.com website. Several friends provided feedback on the various versions of this book: Mary Opalenik, Alex Granzin, Dave Howe, Sakre Edison, Gary Tepfer, and Dixie Feiner. I am particularly grateful for feedback and other support from my wife, Linda, and daughters Berkley and Leah.

I have been a lay member of the Order of Buddhist Contemplatives (OBC) for almost 40 years and a lay minister for the past several years. The OBC is the foundation that has allowed me to write this book. Although I do not explicitly discuss this foundation, the OBC website (http://www.obcon. org) and the Shasta Abbey website (http://www.shastaabbey.org/teachings. html) have numerous books, articles, and free dharma talks that capture the teaching I have received, teaching for which I am deeply grateful. Two OBC monks made special contributions to this book: Rev. Master Meiko Jones read and gave feedback and Rev. Leon Kackman conducted the abbreviated Jukai ceremony for Roy, John, and Cody. My book is not intended to represent the teachings of the OBC, but rather is about my personal practice.

FROM THE CO-AUTHORS

I [am] finally getting a chance to show folks out there that not everybody in prison was solely focused on f–ing up and doing wrong and being negative with our lives. Some of us want to become a better person as best we can with each moment and challenge. Even when we are mistreated, denied medical help by cold and cruelly indifferent people who see us as unworthy of kindness and compassion, some of us still hold to Buddha's teachings. I'm glad people will be able to see Buddha's teachings put into practice within such a setting, a place full of anger, hate violence and death. I know there are lots more men and women in prisons all over the world who believe in loving kindness and compassion and helping others.

—Roy Tester, a. k. a. Saint Badass

All of us came into this world differently but we still have pain and suffering to deal with. We are all human beings and must learn to accept our past life and push forward and spread kindness. This is the saying that just as grass grows, so should our hearts.

As for me, I knew what prison was like and all the stuff you have to deal with, but it did let me know what to look out for and to expect in the future because my other Bros in this book have been doing time for a little while and Ol' Cody is just starting. I loved reading to see what the Bros are doing behind these walls and how they have taken anger and teachings from the professor and let people see our joy and mindfulness.

—Cody Griffin

I cried after reading this. To relive mine and the others' lives through these stories and to read what [Doug Carnine] wrote was the most heart touching feeling ever. It has completed a part of my life I wanted so desperately to share with others in hope to help them transform their lives after hearing of situations my friends and I have and will face. Thank you. In this, my life will help others long after I have gone from this body. This book opens a relationship from the prison world to the outside world. The letters show the path one takes that makes that person's life come to be what it is now. To read a psychology book is not the same as living it. Through these letters you can see and feel these life-changing events.

—John Bruno

[This book] will open eyes and hearts to the truth of prison life and how a few can make a difference in here or out there. Each character in the book is different. Yet one force connects us—kindness and change. Should the book have a warning label? I see warning as a physical preparation but this book is about mental strength. People need awakening sometimes. Let that be the warning. Without pain and suffering there would be no need to practice. I feel for the officers who read this. It will bring a change to their hearts, but not to all of them. One at a time! May an ethical legacy begin!

—Roger "Tad" Price, Jr.

INTRODUCTION

One evening in the spring of 2009, my daughter Leah, home from UC Santa Cruz for a visit, was reading a 40-plus-page letter from a prisoner she was writing to at the Maximum Security Unit located in Tucker, Arkansas, a notorious prison also known as Tucker Max. She would periodically come out of her bedroom, crying. With bloodshot eyes, she talked about how nearly unbearable it was to read about the pain he had been subjected to and had inflicted upon others. She would not allow me to read the letter, saying it was just too disturbing.

Leah was in her 20s at the time, and had been deeply involved in social activism spanning many causes, so my wife and I were hardly surprised that she would be exchanging letters with a convicted murderer. Nor did I find it particularly off-putting when she asked if I would respond to a few of her pen pal's questions about Buddhism. As a lay minister in the Order of Buddhist Contemplatives and a founding member of the Eugene Oregon Buddhist Priory, helping others learn about Buddhism was part of my calling, and I readily agreed.

And so my correspondence with Roy Tester began.

Over the next seven years, I wrote hundreds of letters to Roy and three other prisoners at Tucker Max. Through our correspondence we exchanged ideas about Buddhism, meditation, mindfulness, and kindness. Through our friendship, we deepened our understanding of compassion, humanity, and what it means to be spiritually free. It was a relationship that forever changed all of our lives.

"Person Unknown"

Four years into my correspondence with Roy, my wife, Linda, and I flew to Arkansas to visit him. As my name was called to walk through the metal detector, the clerk standing behind a desk nearby startled me by speaking up. "So you're the man who sends all the books and letters to Roy," she said with a smile. I told her yes, I was, and she remarked that he was lucky to have me helping him out by sending him so much to read.

A few months later, I sent off my usual letter to Roy but for the first time I forgot to include the required identification, "Prisoner #86867," when I addressed the envelope. Even though by now the mail clerk and prison staff had met me in person, knew Roy on a first-name basis, and seen more than 100 letters pass between us, the letter came back, marked "Person Unknown."

In the eyes of the prison, Roy was a number. Only the number could receive the letter, not a person with a name. It wasn't the first time he had been treated like an object rather than as a human being. As a child, Roy had suffered repeated verbal, physical, and sexual abuse at the hands of his father and others, while his mother did nothing to protect him. In adulthood, he was dehumanized by drug and alcohol abuse, and turned to a life of crime. Finally one day in a fight with his parents he killed them both and was sentenced to life in prison.

His first weeks and months in Tucker Max seemed a continuation of the life he lived before. He did drugs, fought with other prisoners, and lashed out at the guards and prison staff, his anger and emotional pain unabated. He had no regard for his own well-being or the well-being of others.

Then one day, something shifted. Walking through his prison barracks, he saw another man sitting very still and quiet, with a calm and peaceful expression on his face. Roy had never seen someone meditating before and he felt an instant pull toward the serenity he felt in the other man. When he approached him later, the man gave him a primer on meditation. Their brief conversation that day started Roy on a path of transformation—a path that gave his spirit freedom and peace, even while his body remained imprisoned in a place many would call hell.

A Life-Changing Partnership

After we were introduced, Roy and I began writing to each other often, with hundreds of letters going back and forth between us in what you might think of as a spiritual conversation. I had never before met anyone like Roy. Setting aside the heinousness of his crime—killing one's own parents is considered one of the few true "sins" in Buddhism—I found him to be genuine, direct, and engaging. His inquiry into Buddhist teaching was at once raw and sophisticated. His reflections on his own past and the reality of his life in prison were honest and unflinching.

Through our letters, I offered instruction on mindfulness, meditation, and Buddhist teachings, and encouraged him as he reached deeper in his practice. Around the same time, in my own life, I had the profound experience of working with a young man who was dying of ALS. Witnessing the grace with which this young man met the end of his life opened my eyes to something that I realized was a missing ingredient that could transform the simple practice of mindfulness and meditation into something truly life-changing: kindness.

The realization was an epiphany. I immediately wrote to Roy about it, and proposed an experiment of sorts. Could he transform not only his own life, but also the lives of his fellow prisoners, by practicing kindness? He responded with enthusiasm, and from that point forward, he dedicated himself to performing kind acts every day—from offering a smile and a kind word to a guard, to buying new shoes for another prisoner, to reading aloud to an illiterate neighbor. After I told a Buddhist friend of mine about this remarkable man, she dubbed him "Saint Badass."

While his acts of kindness had an impact on all who knew him, the most far-reaching effect was on a handful of inmates who became interested in Buddhism and meditation through their relationship with Roy. Over time, Roy introduced them to me, and we began exchanging letters as well.

I nicknamed John Bruno "the thinker" for his abstract and cerebral letters. Roger "Tad" Price was a gifted artist, who once told me that he experienced a sense of transformative awareness and connection while immersed in drawing. Cody Griffin, the youngster, had been suicidal upon arriving in prison, full of rage and despair. With Roy guiding him, Cody turned away from the darkness, and embraced a spiritual practice. One by one, Roy and I expanded our partnership to include each of these men, all new travelers to the path of mindfulness and kindness.

Letters from these men described in gut-wrenching detail the horrific abuse they suffered in childhood, terrible crimes they committed as adults, and the dehumanization of life in prison, where their every waking moment is controlled by others; their few possessions can be searched through or taken at will; real or perceived infractions can result in month-long stints in solitary confinement; and they have no hope of ever sharing a meal with their loved ones again.

Within the prison walls, our partnership became an anchor for each of these men as they faced new hardships, from disabling illness, to attacks at the hands of other prisoners, to family abandonment, to harsh punishments doled out by prison guards. Each prisoner in his own way overcame these struggles, thanks to his growing understanding of mindfulness and kindness.

Our partnership transformed the lives of all four of these men—and me. Although I began as their mentor, over time I came to realize that they, in fact, were teaching me. After years of study, I thought I knew a thing or two about mindfulness and meditation. But not until I saw Roy, John, Tad, and Cody persevere in building kindness out of lives that had experienced and wrought unimaginable cruelty and abuse did I truly understand the deep, transformative power of these practices.

Witnessing their ability to replace anger and despair with compassion and a profound capacity to live in the present moment left me deeply in awe. In turn, I believe that the respect I extended to them helped to smash their belief that they were unlovable, worthless, and despised by society.

Of course, no amount of kindness could change the fundamental reality of prison life for Roy and the others, but their practice still dramatically changed their lives for the better. There were still those staff and inmates who treated Roy with bitterness, cruelty, and anger, but for the first time, he didn't let their attacks control him; he was capable of remaining in control of himself. In fact, he began to see his situation not as a problem, but as an opportunity. He once wrote to me about welcoming the chance to be an example to others, saying, "Hopefully when they see me react to their hatefulness with kindness and compassionate understanding and with Koolness, Buddha's Koolness, it will plant some tiny seed within their hearts."

Eventually I realized that these letters might have the power to teach others the way they had taught me. And that is why I decided to put them together in a book. As a professor of education for 40 years, I had co-authored dozens of textbooks for kindergarten through college-aged students, but I had never written anything as personal as *Saint Badass*. The experience had a profound effect on my own practice and understanding of Buddhism.

By the time I finished the book, I had written the men more than 600 letters, and received far more in return. Their stories of finding heaven within the depths of hell challenged me to question my own grievances and assumptions about my own privileged life, to open my heart to gratitude and kindness, to change my attitudes toward prison reform, and to become an advocate and friend to prisoners. Our partnership has deepened my compassion and understanding for those most marginalized by society, people who are treated as if they were invisible—or worse, trash. Through the partnership, I've gained a new faith in the capacity of every human being to be redeemed and find transcendence, no matter the circumstances.

Of course even the most positive influences of the partnership did nothing to change the fact that these men committed heinous crimes. This book is not an attempt to excuse or whitewash what they did; on the contrary, it shows how the price of their spiritual freedom included acknowledging the impact their actions had upon the world. There is nothing Roy or John or Cody can do to soften the pain and loss for the friends and families of their victims. But I sincerely hope, as I believe they do as well, that reading their stories might inspire others to turn away from violence and selfishness and toward mindfulness and kindness. Their letters might even change your life. I know they changed mine.

About this Book

Most of the content of this book is taken, with permission, from letters and phone conversations between myself and Roy Tester, John Bruno, Cody Griffin, and Roger "Tad" Price, Jr., from 2009 to 2016. The letters and conversations have been edited for length and clarity. Grammar, spelling, and punctuation have been corrected only where necessary for clarification; the original wording has been preserved as much as possible. The glossary defines Buddhist terms you might not familiar with, for example *merit, mala beads, bodhisattva.*

Some names have been changed to protect the privacy of certain individuals. If you become interested in what happens next in the lives of any of my prisoner friends, my blog will include letters they have written after the book was published: http://feedkindness.com/blog/.

A warning to readers: some letters contain explicit language and descriptions of violence, sexual behavior, or abuse. While these passages have been edited to minimize disturbing material, they remain an important part of these men's experiences, and thus have not been excluded from the book.

PART I

a.k.a. SAINT BADASS

CHAPTER 1

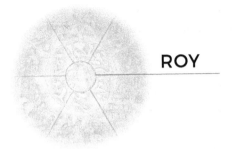

ROY

Name: Roy Tester

Date of Birth: April 1, 1965

Education: 10th Grade, GED

Family: Married three times; one daughter

Prison time: Sentenced in 1999 to life in prison without parole for first-degree murder and capital murder. Previously served a cumulative 11 years on and off for various crimes.

Roy

My life was the result of my crazy childhood. It was totally insane, psychotic shit. Instead of dealing with the shit in my head from childhood, I had run from it, tried to "fog it" with drugs and booze. When I broke it down to cause and effect, when I quit making it personal, it helped. It helped to look at what caused my father to be the way he was, and the same for my mother. Plus, if it hadn't been me, some other kid would have had to experience all that crazy shit. I survived and I broke the cycle of that perversion. I "Let Go," of the burden that had put me on a path of self-destruction for all but the last 10 years of my life.

. . . .

My father was explosive in a 24/7 kind of way. Any little thing would set him off and there was no telling what he would do, how far crazy he was going to get. He threw a running chainsaw at me one time and kicked me through a screen door twice. He tore off the door to our refrigerator and me along with it because I had been holding the door open a second too long, and he went to kicking me up inside of it.

. . . .

My dad bought me a lot of stuff and I think he was trying to say he loved me at times and was trying to "make up" in some way. He just had tremendous confusion in his mind and heart. When your mind and heart aren't in harmony with love and respect and integrity, well, you get all confused and act without thinking, like my dad. Sometimes I would look in his eyes and my dad wasn't there. It may sound crazy, but I know what I saw and didn't see.

. . . .

I was nine years old and my dad had gotten a little crazier than usual and broke my arm and messed my head up a bit. He sent my mom with a pocket full of money to take us to Disneyland in California. I got to be the hero on that one. I knew I was the reason we were going. I was proud of taking that ass kicking so that my brother and sister could go.

. . . .

I recall sitting on the couch eating ice cream. I turn the spoon over (upside down) and just as my tongue touches the ice cream, the spoon is slammed down my throat. Lips, both smashed on my teeth. There was a certain way you were supposed to eat ice cream.

. . . .

Then for my 9th birthday he started the sex bullshit. Yeah, my crazy life and actions were directly influenced by my childhood and its craziness. I would have (I hope) made better decisions, but, I also broke the cycle on the "bullshit." I never put my hands on any kids. Never sexed up any kids. All them guys always crying when they get caught, "My dad did it to me, that's why I did it." Bullshit. They did it because they wanted to. I broke the cycle!

. . . .

On my 10th birthday, my dad walks into the house and puts down his lunch box just as I'm getting some silverware out of the drawer to set the table. I've cooked supper for him, as I do every night. I have to have it ready to eat at 6:00 p.m. You can set your clock by this meal. On this particular day he says, "Happy birthday, you little bastard," and punches me in the mouth with his fist. I have a lifetime scar under my nose down my lip; it's one reason I grow a moustache.

. . . .

Your own father sharing you with a deer-hunting buddy is crazy shit, Bro. It will kind of screw up your head a bit, especially when dear old mom don't do diddly shit to even curb the violence. Nope, her attitude was pretty much: "Just don't bother me, okay?" How do you let your husband do that kind of crazy shit to your son?

. . . .

I think my mother's fear is what had her heart so cold and empty of love and compassion. [My parents] never were overly emotional toward any of us kids. My brother and sister just seemed to accept our parents' behavior as if they had no choice. It was like a houseful of strangers living together.

. . . .

My first personal indoor dog was a black and tan miniature Dachshund given to me by my mom after a particularly brutal beating by my dad. My mom and I went to Conway, about 55 miles away, and I picked him out of three puppies. I looked in the big cardboard box and he looked right in my eyes while the other two were just lying there. I named him Buford and asked him if he wanted to come home with me and he kind of hopped up to stand up on his back legs with his paws on top of the box and I held him and loved him all the way home.

. . . .

To sleep with a critter curled up with you is a special bond. Waking up and looking at him was comforting; after getting a beating he was always there for me, full of love and compassion and understanding. About a month shy of his first birthday, he started losing his balance and getting sick. I took him to the vet and the vet said he would have to be "put down." The vet asked me if I wanted him to kill Buford and I told him I'd kill him and my Grandpa hugged me and we went home. Two days later I went down to my favorite place on a bluff where I went to be alone, where I felt safe, and spent all day playing with and loving and enjoying being with my best friend. Then I shot him and buried him under a pretty, full-blown dogwood tree.

. . . .

Even with all the crazy, hateful, pure meanness I experienced as a kid, whenever I got a bad beating, focusing on caring for all my pets always helped with my pain. When I went to school there were a couple other kids who had mean-ass parents and focusing on them helped too. I'd even sneak food out of our house to feed a couple of my friends because their dads either wouldn't work or when they did, they spent it on booze, so the kids didn't have much of anything.

. . . .

My Granny was my whole world. The last year before her death, dementia was slowly setting in. When she got bad, a cousin called and I flew up with my guitar. I went to her room and started playing her favorite gospel songs and singing to her. Then she called my name and we talked; she was lucid for about 30 minutes. I sat and continued to play off and on for the rest of the day. She would fade in, talk a little then fade out. When it came time for me to leave she whispered, "I love you, baby," and went to sleep. The doctors were trying to understand how she could be lucid so much in one day. I said, "Well, genius, it's all about love."

. . . .

I'm not in contact with any of my family, immediate or otherwise, nor in contact with my dear ol' sis anymore either. We were getting along great, writing every couple of weeks for the first year or so, then, when I asked her to ease off a little on her hellfire and brimstone, fear the Lord God Almighty's wrath for he is a jealous God, and fall on your knees and beg his forgiveness before it's too late, she lost her excitement about us being "family" again, because I wasn't going to be a score for the Christians. Then, when I told her I believed in Buddha's teachings, well, she couldn't deal with that. To her, anything other than her Baptist God is equivalent to devil worship.

. . . .

Strung Out

My dear old father was a crazy, mean alcoholic from his mid-teens onward. He put whiskey in my bottle to keep me quiet when I was a baby. All my uncles and cousins on both sides were alcoholics and drug addicts, so I was a drunk all my life. I could hold some booze by the time I was 12 as well as dope. I did my first shot of meth at age 9 or 10 and you name it, I wanted it. I stayed high and drunk but could function, so to speak. I worked and did good with my grades at school.

This has always been my downfall: go clean for a while, then go crazy; or have the world in my hand and screw it all up. Lots of folks sure try to hide behind dope and booze, saying things like, "Oh, man, I was high and I was drunk or I wouldn't have robbed, raped, or killed." Bullshit! I've been higher than you could ever possibly imagine and I never hid behind it like drugs were an OK excuse. Ain't happening. Don't make it OK.

. . . .

Between the time I left home at 16 years old until I was 19 years old, I went to jail at least 10 times. I was charged with drunk and disorderly conduct, public intoxication, minor in possession, etc. A couple of times I got lucky and blessed to have a smart public defender, but I got arrested on Halloween of 1984 and was in prison by February 1985. I did less than a year and after the first visit to my parole officer I never went back. I just called him and told him to catch up with me. He did—a few weeks later, because I was wasted on booze and drugs and a dude who was on parole who owed me money had called him and told him where to find me.

I did a six-month parole violation, got out, and in less than two weeks was on the run for stealing a motorcycle from a dealership after giving the salesman my driver's license. I was wasted on heroin and mescal and when I woke up the next day by my buddy, the front door was open and I was on the porch, nodding [in and out of consciousness] from heroin. He woke me up, asking where I got the bike and I said, "What bike?" I looked at it, then at him, and still remember him beginning to laugh saying, "You ain't got a clue, do you?" It took another shot of heroin and a few beers and a few swigs of mescal before I finally retraced my movements and figured it out.

I was caught a couple of weeks later, wasted on dope and passed out in a grocery store. I got that plea down to a three-year bit. I did less than a year, got out, and wasn't out six weeks when, while wasted on heroin and whiskey in the middle of the day, I walked into a man's home, loaded up his guns and a pair of boots. Then I fought him over a gun and he won. I got five years for that.

I turned down parole twice on my own. I told them I couldn't handle having a babysitter telling me what I could or couldn't do. I appeared before them twice, talking so crazy I knew they would for sure turn down my parole. I did an extra year and a half so I wouldn't have parole. Then I finally got out the last week of February, 1991.

· · · · · · · ·

I was close to death from hepatitis in 1994. When I regained consciousness, a doctor was looking in my eye with a penlight. She told me, "Mr. Tester, you've been infected with hepatitis, and by the looks of your arms it's from shooting dope. Right?" I blinked my eyes because I didn't have any strength left. I fought to stay awake, and I suddenly got so scared, thinking that if I closed my eyes they'd never open again.

She said, "I'm not going to lie to you or sugarcoat the situation. Your stupidity may have killed you. But if you're still alive tomorrow, still conscious, you'll make it. If you slip into a coma you won't live 48 hours. Your wife's outside and I've already told her, so you might want to say goodbye just in case."

Bro, that was a unique situation to be in. I didn't have years or months. I had a few hours at most. My wife and 10-year-old stepdaughter came in. Both were smiling and trying to be cheerful. I felt like a real piece of shit for causing these two kool, beautiful chicks such pain and sorrow. It was my fault their hearts were being ripped in two. I managed to say, "I'm sorry," and "I love you," before the doctor made them leave. Then I lay there fighting to stay conscious.

I started going backwards, looking at my life and looking at my actions. Did I do more right than wrong? Did I help more than I hurt? Am I a good person? I didn't know what came after death, but I just felt with a certainty that it was crucial to my life essence that I be, in my heart, a good person.

· · · · · · · ·

I remember killing my father. I remember the look in his eyes when he realized it was not going to go down the way it had for years before. But I did not remember I killed my mother for 6 months. When I remembered what I did, I felt like an animal.

· · · · · · · ·

Arkansas Supreme Court

Roy Don Tester vs. State of Arkansas,
Nov. 9, 2000

The bodies of Don and Dana Tester were discovered in their home just outside of London in Pope County on the morning of Saturday, July 18, 1998. It was later determined they had both been strangled; in addition, Dana Tester's throat had been cut. One of their cars, a purple Dodge Stratus, was missing from their home, as were two guns, some of Don Tester's rings and his watch, and Mr. Tester's guitar and guitar case.

The facts that developed at trial reveal the following. Roy Tester went to his parents' home on the morning of Friday, July 17, with [two friends]. After visiting with Mrs. Tester for some time, the three left the house, but returned a few hours later. Tester was inside talking to his mother when his father came inside and asked why Tester had come back. Tester and his father began arguing, and according to [his friend], Tester told his father that "all I wanted to do was give you a hug." As Mr. Tester tried to push his son off of him, [his friend] said, Tester started to choke his father. Mrs. Tester, who had recently had back surgery, was apparently unable to intervene. [His friend] said that a few minutes later, the elder Tester was laying down on the ground; his face was a purplish-brown color, and he was not breathing.

At that point, [the two friends] left the house, but not before they saw that Tester had gone to his mother and had a tight grip on her, holding her down tightly. Some few minutes later, Tester came out of the house with a black guitar case, and the three left the house, [and] drove to Houston, Texas.

While in Houston, Tester confessed to [his friends] that he had killed his parents. According to [his friend], "it was really getting to him ... 'cause he had killed his mom ... , and he said he didn't mind killing his dad, but it really broke him down to kill his mom. It was getting to him that ... he had sliced her throat."

CHAPTER 2

PRISON LIFE

Name: John Bruno

Date of Birth: July 2, 1965

Education: 7th Grade, GED

Family: Married three times; seven children (two deceased)

Prison time: Sentenced in 2003 to life in prison without parole for capital murder. Previously served approximately 16 years for different crimes.

John

It is impossible for anyone to understand confinement that will last until your passing. Not unless one has spent many, many years behind bars and sees the feelings that go with it. To envision something similar, imagine yourself in [a prison like the one described in this chapter]. Now if you can do this for two weeks, you can imagine a lifetime without hope.

Population

"Population" is the place where inmates are allowed to interact, such as at chow call or TV call. Some live together in an open bay, which is a big room with beds/cots about two feet apart. Three toilets sit side-by-side and less than two feet apart with no partitions for privacy. The shower holds up to four at a time.

You must be in Population or you cannot work. Examples of jobs include barracks' clerks and porters, outdoor hoe squad with officers on horseback as overseers, and kitchen labor.

Segregation

Prisoners in "Segregation" [also referred to as "lockdown"] have a single-man cell with a barred door and one 5" x 60" window to let in natural light. There's one toilet-sink combo made of stainless steel, one 2' x 2' steel table for writing and eating, one concrete bench/bed 20" high x 32" wide by 7½' long inside a cell about 7½' wide × 9' deep, counting the concrete slab. In lockdown, no one is allowed outside the cell unless handcuffed and shackled. If someone has physical limitations, then he can be transported in a wheelchair, but still in cuffs and shackles. Twenty hours per day, 54 people are housed in each block and are usually yelling, rapping, singing, beating, banging, and in general making noise close to chaos for about 20 hours a day. Most sleep around 4–5 hours per day.

The Hole

The Hole is punitive isolation where you go for up to 30 days at a time to be punished for breaking a rule. It consists of a nasty single-man cell with a bar cell door reinforced by another, solid door so that you can't see anyone walking past the cells. The mattress is 3⅝ inches thick and is available only at night. There is no TV, no radio, or [visits to the] library.

. . . .

If you go outside, they take you to a 10 x 15 cage like a dog kennel and lock you in for one hour. You cannot take your clothes off no matter how hot it gets. When your time is up you must strip down completely in front of everyone, get shackled and handcuffed again, and brought back to your cell. If you go to the infirmary you must walk handcuffed and shackled after you are strip searched and again your cell is searched.

Possessions

Population and Segregation have what is given to them by the state and items "privileged" them by the Commissary. You receive a toothbrush 3 inches long with clear toothpaste, 2 bars of lye soap, 2 rolls of toilet tissue, 1 face towel, 1 towel, 1 laundry bag, 2 pair of white boxer shorts, and in winter you receive 2 pair of thermal tops and bottoms. Your bedding is 1 blanket,

2 sheets, 1 pillowcase, 1 foam mat with a plastic cover and a thin, green pillow. Your property box is a 32-gallon, rectangular clear box. You have 1 pair of canvas shoes that are blue and 1 pair of work boots, plus 3 pair of state issued shirts and pants that have no pockets except for one on the left back of the pants.

Everything must fit inside your box, including allowable items such as radios, medical prescriptions, headphones, ear buds, and books. You cannot put anything on your door, walls, ceiling, window, or bars. Nothing may be on your table unless you are writing a letter or doing law work. You may not cover your light or put your blanket on the floor (a blanket on the floor is considered misuse of State property). Cell phones, dope, cigarettes, green money [cash], or any item pertaining to consumption of drugs such as a pipe for smoking is contraband.

When you go to Isolation [the Hole], your allotted possessions change. You receive 1 soap, 1 toothpaste, and 1 toothbrush. Clothes are limited to 2 t-shirts, 1 jumpsuit, 2 pairs of socks, 2 boxers (in winter two additional sets of thermal tops and bottoms). You may have only one Bible or religious book, a pen, stamped envelopes, and writing tablet. You get only ½ roll of tissue three times a week. There's no pillow, 1 blanket in summer and 2 in winter, 2 sheets, 1 towel, 1 washcloth, and 1 laundry bag. You may not have pictures, personal books, dictionaries, or anything else.

The Commissary

Each barracks has a different commissary day. Population gets two days a week, while Segregation and the Hole get only one day a week. Pens, writing tablets, and envelopes are the only options for those in the Hole/Isolation. Segregation can get other items such as sodas and V-8 juice, but razors and fudge bars are privileged.

Chow

At 1:30 a.m. count time is started. The Sergeants who supervise the barracks take the inmate porters to the chow hall and pick up four large containers (two for coffee, one for milk, and one for juice). This is done every morning for barracks five, six, seven, and eight, which are in segregated lockdown. There are 54 people per barracks, a total of 208 single man cells. Each barracks gets two plastic serving pitchers to pass out drinks to each inmate. Now, by the time this is done, it is time for everyone to go back down the hallway to pick up the food carts. By 3:30 a.m. the food is distributed. You get only 10–15 minutes to eat before they come and pick up the tray. By 4:30 a.m. all the trays are picked up, the trash picked up, and the floors swept and mopped. Then the porter leaves.

The same actions are repeated for lunch and dinner, except that the four jugs have Kool-Aid one day and tea the next day. Lunch is served between 9:00 a.m.–11:00 a.m. and dinner between 2:00 p.m.–4:00 p.m. Then we starve until breakfast.

Personal Hygiene

Population has showers every day. Segregation and Isolation get only three 10-minute showers per week. As no one in Segregation or Isolation is allowed a razor, an inmate barber shaves you three times a week. Population gets haircuts once a week, while Isolation gets a haircut twice a month. Except for those in Population, inmates are handcuffed and shackled while going to and from the cell to the showers.

Entertainment

Inmates are limited to three books on a once-a-week visit to the library. Those in Isolation get nothing. You get a small Sony radio with ear buds and a TV that comes on at 4:30 p.m. and goes off at 10:30 p.m.

Population sees movies all day Saturday and Sunday, and Friday night. Segregation can only watch one movie, scheduled Friday night at 9:00 p.m., and watch the same movie again at 7:00 a.m. Saturday and Sunday mornings. Isolation does not see movies.

Physical Activity

Segregation and Isolation have recreation call one hour a day, five days a week, to go to a [chain link] cyclone cage with a concrete floor that has a cage-like opening on the top to let in the air from outside. You are escorted there and back in handcuffs and leg shackles. The recreation area for Population is 50 feet by 250 feet. Population is divided according to housing barracks and rotated according to particular sports such as volleyball, kickball, or baseball tosses. There is no bat. There are no horseshoes. Bats and horseshoes are considered weapons. There's also a gym for handball and basketball. Those in Population participate in holiday games such as chess, bingo, and team volleyball, and the winners receive prize money.

Shakedown

Guards enter your cell and tell you to strip down, followed by redressing and shackling. You then stand outside your cell while the guards search everything inside the cell including letters and books and the seams on your mattress and pillow, looking for contraband. The contents of your property box are dumped out. This is all done to provoke you into an outburst so they can write you up for a rule infraction or beat you down, called "restraining the inmate."

Strip Search

A strip search means taking off your clothes one item at a time and handing it to an officer for them to physically feel the article for possible contraband. You strip until you are completely naked then open your mouth, lift your tongue, and finally lift your privates. You then must squat and cough three times. If the guards are hostile they make you turn around and bend over then use your hands to spread your butt cheeks. If they are feeling ugly they yell at you to spread them wider. It's a form of harassment and intimidation. You can be ordered to get dressed, then to be stripped all over again.

Desires

I spend my day walking or reading and meditating continuously and keep my mind in the outside world. But, this is my life for the next 40 to 50 years. I got 25 years already behind bars and haven't touched a woman in 15 years. These women [visitors] run around with perfume and pants so tight you can see everything. Crazy! But if we get caught playing with ourselves we go to the Hole for 30 days. I'm 49 years old and can't satisfy myself with a fantasy.

The Guards

If it was not for the guards, there would be no drugs, green money, cell phones, or anything illegal. Just last night a guard sat and talked to me while the porter lit a cigarette for the inmate in the cell next to me. It might not seem bad, except that no tobacco is allowed. The guards are supposed to shake the inmates down or bust them for doing wrong but you know why they don't? If they did, they would be writing disciplinary reports all day long. When the guards see who has money, they leave them alone and bust the nobodies instead. You have a total of thirty guards per 12-hour shift. That's four separate shifts. They work two days on and three days off or three days on and two days off. There are a total of 592 inmates in this unit. An inmate deals with one guard at a time. The guards deal with 216–300 inmates a day, every day. What's the old war tactic? Overwhelm with numbers. Now if they feel like getting down and dirty they enforce the regulations and can make it worse on us.

Classification

In this book, when prisoners mention their "class," they are usually refer-ring to their "good time classification." Within the Arkansas Department of Corrections, a committee reviews each inmate and awards them Class 1, 2, 3, or 4 status. Inmates receive special privileges according to their status, and their class can be lowered as a disciplinary measure or raised for good behavior. Inmates in isolation must maintain Class 1 status in order to return to the general population and Class 1 prisoners are also eligible for more desir-able jobs.

There is a second classification system for prison employment. John explains:

Class C is for those who cannot work outside the fence unless under armed guard. Class B is for those who can work outside the fence without armed guards. Class A is for special inmates, such as those who drive the semi-trucks with goods to each penitentiary from the central office in Pine Bluff, or those who live in a free world house with the dogs that hunt other inmates down. They are considered traitors. Personally, I don't care. I put myself here, not them.

Solitary

I went to Classification and this is what they said. I will be in Class 4 for a year, which means I will not be eligible to get out of here [the Hole] for 15 months. This is their reasoning: 1. Inmate has rebellious and aggressive conduct, behavior, and attitude. 2. Inmate indicates a "chronic" inability to comply with agency rules and regulations and is a threat to the agency mission. All of this because I won't kiss their … I treat all officers with respect and treat all inmates with respect. I just will not bow down to rules that take a man's manhood from him to where they want you to become their slave. I have not, am not, and will not worship or be a slave to any man. They hate the fact that they have tried everything to break my spirit. I have been in the Hole 38 times and still I come out smiling with thank you and you're welcome. Boy it makes them mad. 1,140 days in solitary and I'm more jovial every time. Most are starting to believe I'm crazy.

CHAPTER 3

"TRY BREATHING"

Roy

I was going to the bathroom to get high and kick it with some fellow addicts when, as I was walking up the aisle, I saw this huge dude sitting half lotus with a serene look on his face. I had noticed him because it was impossible not to. I remember saying, "What the f–!" as I walked past and went on to the bathroom to get high and kicked it for a good 15 minutes, then something just pulled me back over towards him because I lived on the opposite wall up near the front.

The dude is at least 6' 4" and easily 300 lbs., yet I walked right up to him. I guess it was to show him I wasn't scared of him. Then I looked up at him and asked, "What the f– were you doing a while ago?" He just smiled an easy, comfortable smile and dug around in his box until out came a meditation primer. He said to me, "Man, I know you read a lot. Check this out. Try breathing, focusing on your breath, then try it for at least 10 minutes, but it's even better if you go 15 minutes every day." He emphasized "every day." He said, "It's quieter in the morning and I noticed you're always up after breakfast until work call. Try it at least once a day for 30 days and you'll never stop."

He still had such a f–ing relaxed, totally peaceful look on his face and a relaxed body. It's a madhouse after work call is over because construction and maintenance crews are all in showering, getting high, and drinking bootleg booze while winding down, yet he was totally relaxed and unaffected by the craziness around him.

. . . .

I was thinking I needed to check this shit out because time sure ain't shit for him. I took the book and started reading it. As I never was much for TV, I had plenty of time to absorb the book's knowledge. He was right. After 30 days I couldn't quit.

. . . .

I don't remember the name of the second book he gave me, but I do remember the Noble Eightfold Path and Four Noble Truths took up the first half of it.

It wasn't long after that I started changing things in my life in a positive way. I even had some guys accuse me of trying to run a scam. That struck me as kind of silly and I asked them to tell me how studying Buddhism and meditating even when I was bone-weary tired or sick was a scam or why changing some of my negative ways, like shooting dope in my arms or hustling dope to make money to survive in prison, was a scam. They couldn't think of anything to say.

The Gentle Giant gave me a resource directory [of Buddhist organizations] after I started asking him about the Dharma. I hustled up 20 or 25 stamped envelopes and started writing, asking for help for a new recruit. I asked for the Dhammapada [a collection of Buddhist scriptures] or something that would be good for someone just starting to sit, and anything that would help my practice to grow. I got about a 75 percent return on the mail project and that's how I found out about Bo and Sita Lozoff and the Human Kindness Foundation Prison Ashram Project. It's been a road I'm definitely glad I decided to drive down.

I wrote my first letter to Roy on November 17, 2009, after my daughter Leah put us in touch. We quickly bonded over our common interest in Buddhist practice. As I learned more about Roy's life, I became determined to find a focus for our partnership that would be powerful enough to lift Roy out of his feelings of guilt and despair, and help him not only change himself but also improve the lives of those around him.

Doug

I am the father of Leah and a Buddhist lay minister. Leah said you had questions about Buddhism. I know what you have written her has touched her deeply. Please feel free to write me about Buddhism. I believe that your Buddhist practice would also help me deepen my practice, so any correspondence would be of use to me as well. I am retired and about 17 months ago developed problems with my hip, back, and shoulder that for the first time in my life limited what I could do and also made pain a fairly constant companion. I found that this setback has been a challenge to my Buddhist practice; I spend too much time wrapped up in myself—the small self. I have so much to be grateful for that it is disappointing to be so self-centered.

If there are Buddhist books you would like to receive, please let me know the titles. I can also recommend some titles. I look forward to hearing from you.

Roy

Hey-n-Hello to you

May peace, Happiness, and good health be with you and all sentient beings. ☺

Soon as I saw the Eugene, Oregon address I knew you're in some way connected to Leahjo☺ Hearing from you and learning you are a Buddhist lay minister is way beyond kool and awesome☺ Leahjo had told me her folks were Buddhists and she had grown up with Buddhism☺ She seems to be a very kool person with her head on right. She cares about other people, critters, and the earth that mankind seems to want to destroy with so much pollution, stripping, and basically raping in a savage way. Yeah, I had a pretty "krazy" childhood and a way beyond normal life, which in a large way contributed to my being in prison with a life without parole sentence. I feel the "System" really did a number on me. I refuse to dwell on it. It is what it is, and no matter what, I'm determined to keep pushin' on. Crying, bitching, and whining just make it worse.

Hell, I have it better in prison than millions upon millions of people on this earth. Three meals every day, not too tasty, but meals nonetheless, except on federal holidays when we are blessed with only two meals, but like I said I eat every day. I have medical problems, and you have to force them to help you, but I've got it better than millions.

In a way, I'm in a monastery except for the noise. Once you get the hang of it you can pretty much "block out" the noise and learn to get full use of the quiet times. They are precious. Sometimes though, it is easier for me to "Groove" when the guys are in full form, as in excited about a football game and slamming dominoes. Sometimes the quiet times, well, sometimes the quietness is too loud. Yeah, oxymoron, but I am sure you know what I mean.

I know and feel you on the physical uncoolness. My wild and krazy life has given my body some punishment—several broken bones and other dweebage [troubles] that tries to defy my wish to Groove. Most aggravating of all is the fusion surgery in my back. [The pain] tries to interfere, but it is the very key to helping me "tune out" all the madness and "tune in" to "just chillin'."

I have to catch myself though on an unkoolness. Something I hope you can help me with is my judging of others. I catch myself looking at others in the chow hall or anywhere. I think to myself: that one is a child molester, that one is a raper, that one is a slimy weasel, etc. Then I'm like, damn it, I'm judging their behavior and actions. It's a major aggravation here lately.

Yeah, I know, take the log out of my own eye before I look at the splinter in another's eye. I'm a firm believer that your character, behavior, and actions define who you are. I would appreciate some guidance with judging. How do I get to where I can just accept people for who they are? Any kind of material/advice is more than welcome. Also, what about purifying negative karma? See, I killed my parents and I've read a couple of different times in the many, many books about Buddhism that my crime, killing my parents, is beyond bad. It is the worst crime one can commit.

If Leahjo still has the letter where I told her about my "life" from childhood up; well, if you were to read it I think you could maybe understand the "why" behind my "snapping" and killing my parents. If you could hook me up with some guidance there I'd appreciate it.

I "feel you" on the wrapped up in Self. Seems I catch myself in that so much, as I do in judging others. Does the fact that I'm aware of these dweebs [troubles] mean that I've got a head start in making positive changes?

The longer I sit to write or read or Groove the more I do battle with the physical pain. Sometimes I win, sometimes I lose only to get back up and try again. Can't do a full lotus but a kind of half lotus, depending on the weather and whether or not my knee and back want to cooperate.

I'm damn sure not going to "tap out" [suicide]. I shall endeavor to persevere! I told Leahjo that "a puny effort produces measly results." In a way I like the battle—the obstacles, the noise, the asshole holier than thou guards with major chips on their shoulders, the aches-n-pains of my physical dweebs— the casual everyday chaos. When I "come out" of "Groovin'" and come back to now, I feel, well, kind of happy that I won a battle. The Path [continuing to practice mindfulness and kindness] is a series of battles that I'm determined to win. I look back on when I started Groovin' with Buddhism and have come a long way since 2002. Got lots and lots of more Groovin' to do, lots of "de-dweebing" [troubleshooting] to do, and that means I sure as hell ain't bored! Got more time and opportunity to Groove than y'all free world folks. Just got to make the best of whatever situation you find yourself in. So far as "material," well, anything, books, magazines, pamphlets, etc., I'm more than grateful for. I'm always ready for input.

Always go to sleep with Groovin' on material. Wake up, trying from the start to be a decent person, trying to be a good Buddhist. Hit rough spots, bump up against walls, but "I keep pushin' on." Nothing worth a damn is easy. Just have to "cowboy up" and Groove. When I bump up against a wall I find a way over or around it. Any advice you can give on Groovin' on the Path, well, I'm ready to check it out. Hope you can find a way to neutralize the unkoolness of that physical aggravation you got trying to distract you. I feel you on that. If I ever thought I'd live past thirty I would have taken a lot better care of my body☺ I'm forty-four now but got lots of miles left. What time I do have left is going to be spent trying to get right, trying to be a good "Buddha Wannabe."

Also, need help with "just chill" because I find myself getting aggravated and mentally taking sides on shit that ain't none of my business and don't concern me at all. Help me fight distractions. Okay, really gone this time.

Doug

After reading your letter, I think you might be of more help to me than I can be to you. Let's see!

Here are the parts of your letter that are important teachings for me.

1. Refusing to dwell on what's negative about your life. Instead "I'm determined to keep pushing on."

2. Recognizing that in a way you are in a monastery (except for the noise).

3. The pain from your back "… is the very key to helping me 'tune out' all the madness and 'tune in' to 'just chillin'.'" This response to pain is one of the most important things I hope to learn.

4. "A puny effort produces measly results."

5. "I sure as hell ain't bored."

6. "I like the battle." There is an important aspect of Tibetan Buddhism that is based on the warrior in carrying out the practice. I am thinking of a book for you that talks about this: *When Things Fall Apart* [Chödrön, 2002].

Now I'll turn to your questions and places where I have comments.

1. "… sometimes the quiet is too loud," and judging others and "getting aggravated and mentally taking sides on shit that ain't none of my business …" These are all problems for me too. I have combined them here because I try to deal with all of them in the same way—mindfulness, which leads to letting go. Letting go of the too quiet, the judging, and being caught up in other people's business. I have found these two words in Buddhism—letting go—to be exceedingly difficult for me to act on. Here are some of the actions I have taken (and am still working on):

   a. Seeing each person as the Buddha, which is in fact true. This is hard for me to do.

   b. More recently I have reminded myself that this moment is actually my entire life—the past and future are just thoughts in my mind. Given that this moment is all I am—all the entire world is—I think about how I want my life to be. Do I want to be angry? Do I want to be judging?

   c. The way I want my life to be is to be of service to others, to be grateful. These are feelings you write about. I call up these feelings immediately after I realize this moment is my entire life.

   d. Mental acts such as calling up gratitude and thinking of how to be of service often do not free me from judging.

e. I am now also adding a physical component. I touch my thumbs together as if in seated meditation or even just touch the tip of my thumb to the tip of my first finger or feel the material of my shirt or any other physical sensation.

2. Killing your parents. Buddha told Angulimala [a murderer who gave up violence after converting to Buddhism] that he was cleansing his karma and would continue for the rest of his life. Because someone who had murdered almost 1000 people was able to cleanse his karma, I believe you can cleanse yours, but doing so will not be easy or swift. Cease from evil, do only good, do good for others.

3. Sitting in full lotus. I have never been able to sit in full lotus. I sat in half lotus for a few years, but mostly Burmese lotus—legs on the floor, one leg in front of the other. For the past two years I have been sitting in a chair. My posture is poor—that is the problem, not where I sit. I suggest you pay attention to sitting up straight, leaning neither forward nor backward, nor side-to-side.

I hope this letter serves you well. Your letter has benefited me.

As Roy and I exchanged letters I began to grasp his despair—memories of his childhood abuse, guilt from murdering his parents, impairments and pain from his broken back, and a future in prison that would continue until death. Our give-and-take about meditation seemed inadequate to trigger a dramatic change in his outlook on life.

Then I thought about Roy's desire to be of service to others, which is a form of kindness. Although Buddhism in the West usually focuses on wisdom through meditation and mindfulness, kindness is also an important part of the practice. While I'd witnessed and tried to practice kindness throughout my life, it was my experience as a hospice volunteer that made me think kindness might be the key to unlocking Roy's potential to transform his life.

Jeremy was a 35-year-old ALS patient in hospice care. A deeply spiritual yoga practitioner, Jeremy had lost 60 pounds of muscle mass in the past six months and had no use of his body below his neck, yet he radiated joy and kindness. Even before his devastating diagnosis, Jeremy had faced many personal difficulties and yet he spoke of his life with nothing but gratitude.

In reflecting upon his death, Jeremy sometimes described himself as just a drop of water in a waterfall. He had come from a great river and in a short time, to that river he would return. "Everything is part of me and I am part of everything," he once told me. "All of life is precious, very precious. As long as I live I want to be a positive force, a light full of love for my people, which is everyone. It does not make any difference what kind of water drop you are; you could be any shape, any size, or any color. You are all the same as I am. And I am the same as you. I am a very blessed individual to have had so much time to be able to feel and smell, to be able to run, and love and laugh and hurt."

Jeremy did not waste time on self-pity. With virtually no control of his body or the external world, his kindness poured forth endlessly. Its effect was magnetic. Another hospice volunteer called me to ask if she could visit Jeremy, just to be in his presence. Workers at the care facility would sit with Jeremy when they had a break. In the weeks before he died, I saw in Jeremy living proof that combining meditation and kindness had unbelievable power—enough power, I believed, to transform Roy. I decided to invite Roy to join me in practicing kindness along with mindfulness. He accepted eagerly, and our partnership was born. I had no idea if anything would come of this experiment, but I sent Roy a small amount of money to buy food and supplies to share with other prisoners.

Doug

I have a question for you. I sent the extra money to see if this crazy idea of mine might be possible: Because I (and you) would like to encourage kindness in the world, would it be possible for you to give money, stamps, or food, etc. to prisoners you see being kind? You could say a person writing you asked you to do this. If encouraging kindness turns out to be possible, I can send more funds later. As you can see, I trust you.

CHAPTER 4

BUDDHA DUDE

Roy

Just read one of the most awesome books of all time; it's His Holiness the Dalai Lama's newest book, *Ethics for the New Millennium*. Totally a without a doubt, a WOW! It's the kind of book that you can feel as you read. On the last page, his last words are a prayer that I feel every time I recite them:

> *May I become at all times, both now and forever*
> *A protector for those without protection*
> *A guide for those who have lost their way*
> *A ship for those with oceans to cross*
> *A bridge for those with rivers to cross*
> *A sanctuary for those in danger*
> *A lamp for those without light*
> *A place of refuge for those who lack shelter*
> *And a Servant to all in need.*

I can't help but feel that! It is now added to my practice and it helps get me fired up every morning. Added to my adapted Loving-kindness meditation is this: "May all beings know how it feels to be cared about, may they know that I care."

....

Hey, almost forgot to share the Koolness from a Christian group today. They paid to have a meal catered in: BBQ Brisket, baked beans with chunks of brisket in them, two dill slices, two slices of free-world bread, and a cup of vanilla ice cream with chocolate syrup and chopped nuts. And some bad-ass ice cold lemonade. And they played about 10 minutes of live bluegrass Gospel music. Very Kool. Gave a short, little uplifting message about Love being the answer and there was no separation between man and God. Bro, there's about 600 people here. That's a nice check to pick up. A lot of love and kindness, active kindness. Not just sitting in church praying for our wayward souls, but coming down and feeding us and not just with food but with loving-kindness.

. . . .

I fell off my cushion of "I'm doin' okay." They moved in a child molester, right above me, and he got to describing how he treated some of his victims, how many different mean things he did, getting explicit and enjoying every word. I snapped and screamed real loud, a scream of rage and everything got super quiet. I was consumed with murderous rage, picturing myself dashing this cho-mo child molester with a bucket of paint thinner or boiling water with ammonia. I was violently angry. Then I saw what I was doing and looked around. We're all in individual cells. I felt as though I had actually thrown that bucket of paint thinner and set him on fire or that I had actually thrown that boiling ammonia.

My friend, I haven't experienced that kind of rage in forever. So much for being in control. Well, I apologized to the guy and after he laughed, he said, "Yeah whatever," but he stopped doing all the verbal descriptions. He was only in the cell two more days but he stayed quiet, which was unlike him.

. . . .

[The Buddhist teaching] "Our afflictions are wisdom in disguise" is as real as you can get. Throughout my life, my afflictions have been what helped me to reach and teach others who have been through much of the same kinds of hell on earth. Who better to reach out to someone who has been abused in a monstrous way than someone else who has overcome the same crazy shit?

I can't help but pass judgment on myself when I f– up. I know I am supposed to just observe, reside in a non-judgmental awareness at all times. Passing judgment on myself is counterproductive to growing in my practice and is attachment. But after some time has passed I realize, or rather remember, that I'm supposed to just observe, like sitting in meditation as thoughts arise. Instead of attaching to a thought, just let it go. Instead of passing judgment on myself, notice I've f–ed up, regret, sincerely regret, and, like making a wrong turn while traveling, make the proper adjustment so that I don't commit the same mistake: get back on track.

. . . .

A friend just brought me a cup full of peanut butter he sneaked from the kitchen. A guard asked him why he brought me the peanut butter and he said because I always make him feel better. [The guard] said every time he comes by my cell I'm always smiling and upbeat. He said even when he knows I'm in pain I'm not bitching or complaining about any and every little f–ing thing. He said, "Tester, you've got life without [parole], but you act like you're a short timer fixing to go home."

. . . .

More and more guys in here are finding themselves alone, as in their people are cutting them loose. Times out there are getting harder and harder to survive, so they're cutting expenses and slowly pulling back from the family in prison. I know four guys that have been cut loose so to speak. Their families don't answer the phone; they have them blocked. They don't write any more.

I know one black guy, one Mexican, and two white guys whose people have said, "F– 'em." They've all got life or life without parole. The white guys are both borderline illiterate and thrive on Jerry Springer and Maury Povich. They're just hicks and regret they are so f–'ed up in the head. They know they are ignorant, not bright at all, but when I talk to them their hearts are crushed that their families have just said "F– 'em." They aren't asking for money, just an "I still love you" postcard. I've seen friends stick by friends in here better than so-called family. It's always been a place where the occasional "Dear John" letter shows up but the last couple of years it's enough to be shocking. You can hear the hurt and loneliness in their voices.

Sacks of Kindness

I would like to, "with your Blessing," put together approximately 12–15 "Sacks of Kindness." There are 12 fellas in here that have no one sending them a hello or good-bye or anything, so I'd like for us to help out with some kindness and let them know someone cares. I know what each one needs plus I know these fellas pretty much. Maybe around the 8th of December you can put some more money on my account so I can get the miscellaneous stuff, like t-shirts or whatever. There are some notes in with this stuff, shower shoes, etc. Does the "Sacks of Kindness" idea sound OK/kool by y'all? I have a couple of officers on each shift who "gave it their blessing" and will help get everything where it needs to go. This is more kindness than most of these fellas have experienced in four years or more. This prison, well, there are some really good guys in here—generous and kind—but just not a lot of them. There are at least two or three guys in any block you go to that are "out of it," gone. They don't have anything: a soup bowl, a toothbrush, or bar soap. They have no will; the light in their eyes has gone out.

. . . .

Bro, we've got the blessing for this idea—"Sacks of Kindness"—from a used-to-be asshole [guard], but kindness has really begun to change him. He will help get the Sacks throughout the cell block. It's a sign. Well, guess I'll go, so Let Go-n-Let Kindness Grow. There's joy everywhere!

. . . .

My sister sent me some pesos for my birthday. She said to make it last. Whatever. I got two boxes of Frosted Flakes, two bags of Cheerios, nine honeybuns and jam, and served breakfast to The Fellas, who are the mental health guys and the castaways. I gathered up all their bowls, washed them, then filled up their bowls with their cereal preferences and mixed up some powdered milk. I sliced the wrappers on the big honeybuns, "jammed" them with the strawberry jam and set that on top of their lids. I got an awesome, Kool feeling with every look on their faces as I served them breakfast. They looked at me like, "Wow, someone f–ing cares," and I felt so wowed myself to be able to show them that someone does care about them. After our breakfast I hooked them all up with a couple of good shots of coffee and it was a Kool Happening. The sad thing is my sister would dweeb if I told her how much I spent on the breakfast for The Fellas. Anyway, it was a great way to spend my b-day pesos.

. . . .

My neighbor in #13 is Floyd. He has that real bad rheumatoid arthritis with his fingers and thumbs messed up bad. It is difficult for him to do stuff like fix a meal so I shake up a jug of breakfast drink and slide it over to him with a couple of granola bars or strawberry jam-n-peanut butter mixed up together. Or I write a letter to his only kin alive that we know of, or to a pen pal place. I send over my Buddhist magazines and he says, "Appreciate ya, feller, and tell the Buddha Man [Doug] I appreciate him too."

I tried to tell him I wasn't always a Buddha dude. He said even when he first met me when I was wild n crazy I still helped out guys, but now I'm just able to do it more often. He said the reason we're able to do it is because we could do it and did do it and liked doing it. He keeps the youngster occupied when he realizes I'm trying to study/practice.

· · · · · · · ·

The 20-year-old kid is "skitzed" on Ritalin, a handful of other "child controller" chemicals [he has taken] since he was 5, and all kinds of chemicals from his strung-out parents. Kid bounces off the walls 20 hours a day for 3–4 days then sleeps 12 hours for a couple [days] then back to bouncing off the walls, practically skitzed in his speech, no ability to focus for more than 15 minutes on any one thing. Asks a million questions a day. No one ever told him he could figure out a LOT of stuff on his own. Left to raise his self since birth. Not a bad youngster, just never had any schooling on regular school stuff nor anyone schooling him on how to be a good person.

The skitzed youngster finally built himself into a full-tilt frenzy, screaming and ricocheting off the door. They ended up extracting him and those actions can get physical to different degrees. He didn't weigh 135 lbs., but it took four 300-pounders to get him hog-tied. He had been worked up for about seven hours, up to the moment he blew his top and snapped; all this time I was talking nonstop to him in a soothing, calming tone. I never tried so hard to reach somebody, Bro. I haven't really a clue as to what all I said to him. In the end it didn't work. I would still try again though, partner! I would like to think everyone would.

CHAPTER 5

A GOOD KIND OF HAPPY

Roy

Hey, my neighbor on the left just hollered at me and said. "Hey man, ain't you one of them Buddha dudes? What's that stuff all about? Y'all be sitting Injun-style and got your eyes closed but what y'all doing? Prayin' or meditatin' or something?" I told him, "Hang on Bro, I'll be back in a minute and kick it with you about Buddhism and meditation!" "That's kool, Bro. Knew I'd been hanging on to this book *Beginner's Guide to Meditation* for a reason." Well, gonna go kick it with the dude about us Buddha dudes.

. . . .

Next, had a good "kickin' it" with my neighbor. He was really grooving on everything when I got through. It made all the suffering I've experienced in this block mean something. To suffer needlessly is one thing, but for something good to come of it well, I'll suffer if someone can be helped because of it. Nuttin' 2it.

. . . .

The neighbor in the other block, the one interested in Buddhism and meditation, sent the book back with a note asking if he could borrow it again sometime so he could learn some more about it. I immediately sent it back with a reminder that I had given the book to him in the first place and I would continue to help him with his practice as long as he wanted me to, which means that I'd be sharing more material with him and would never leave him hanging. I would not run out on him. If I couldn't answer his questions, I'd do everything in my power to get the answers for him.

That was at breakfast. Just a few minutes ago I got another kite [a message passed from prisoner to prisoner, not officially allowed]. He's just blown away by that, Bro, and said he was wishing he'd found out about Buddha a long time ago. He said I acted like I didn't know he was black. So I'm going to articulate my thoughts and shoot him a kite tomorrow. I have to let him know love and truth and the Buddha's teaching totally transcend color and nationality and gender.

· · · · · · · ·

On my left is a young white guy, who got a boatload of time—that means thirty or more years. Anyway, I hear him cussing. "F– man! Why me, Goddammit?!" So I call over, "Hey, young feller, ya alright? What's up with ya? Anything I can help ya with? Shit, never know. Ol ' feller like me might just be able to do something or help you figure out something. Or ya can just tell me to mind my own f–in' business."

He says, "Well no, Old School, ain't no problem with you trying to help. I'm just stupid because I can't f–in' read, man. Tried a million times. Just can't. Never would stay in school so I f–'ed myself up and ain't never learned nothing so I'm f–in' stupid and I got a letter today and don't know who it's from." So I stop him and say, "Sheeit young feller, I'd be happy to 'handle up' on reading your mail to you. Slide that rascal on over here and I'll hook you up. They call me Roy or Old School or Tester." Then I read his mail to him.

· · · · · · · ·

And oh yeah, they put this kid in next to me in the corner. He was just savagely beaten and raped and is a bit of a mess in his mind. His family has pretty much abandoned him. I've been spending a lot of time talking with him, listening to him. Caring. He ain't really had much of that, especially from any family. He has meditated a little, is trying and I've been sharing some material with him.

I told him about you because he asked why I was helping him. Why did I care and why did I share my story with him. Cases like this kid, Bro, it breaks my heart. Well, I can't not help people, Bro, and I know you're the same. Kindness is just so alien to this kid so please send him some healing merit [Buddhist positive energy]. We'll get him better together! I appreciate your help so much. Your kindness helps me to help others and spread kindness; being kind helps my pain too. Kid's name is Dustin. Can't barely read, well, not much more than probably 4th or 5th grade level and I don't like the word retarded, but he is really challenged mentally.

· · · · · · · ·

The kid Dustin got some mail earlier. Dig this, from his Mom! I read it for him and it was a beautiful letter. His mom had left his abusive father, filed for divorce, has begun to get her shit together. She begged his forgiveness for not being a good mother, for letting all the abuse go on, etc. She is coming to visit if he says okay. She sent him 50 dollars and asked if he needs anything, books, anything. He smiled and cried and I did too. I'm so happy for him.

He asked me to "read some more Buddha" to him afterwards. He just got calm when I read to him about the Buddha. He seems to "understand." When I read the Noble Eightfold Path, it gave a brief but clear explanation of each step and he really seemed to understand each one. I mean, to hear him talk and to watch him as he usually reacted to everything, you wouldn't think he could comprehend much. But it was like he all of a sudden had a higher I.Q. or a much deeper comprehension level when I started talking to him about Buddhism. It was a total surprise and kind of hard to explain.

Then he wanted to make out a store list and he said he wanted to "pay me back" for what I did for him. I had to bring things to a stop there and explain why my kindness didn't work like that. I explained again real kindness and compassion and gave you as an example, and even though I had told him about you before, this time it was like he could "see" what I meant. It was kind of difficult to explain this whole scene but it was Kool.

· · · · · · · ·

I'm trying to find some kind of regular novel to share with Old Shasif, the Iranian down the tier. I've known him for many years. He's not very sociable, not into idle chit chat. He's just anti-social, not hateful or anything. We ain't got to talk a lot to be friends. Old Shasif knows that if he needs something or some help or favor, all he has to do is shoot me a kite and I'll handle it or help him if I can. Likewise, if I need to remember a book or ask an off the wall question, he usually knows. You'd be surprised at the encyclopedias he's read. Oh, hey Bro, that reminds me, I've been meaning to ask you if you know where to get an address for a world almanac? I want to write and ask them if they'll sell me a damaged copy. Or you could find out on the computer what they charge for the current world almanac. They have like a zillion facts in them. Shasif already knows a lot of stuff, but it would really please him greatly.

Out of all his family, he's got one grandson who writes to him at all. It's sad that they've pretty much run out on him. It happens to quite a few of these guys. Outta sight is outta mind.

· · · · · · · ·

I've been sending stuff you write on Mindfulness and [Shasif] says that you're a good person with a good mind. He still has a heavy accent. It's kool to listen to him talk. He's a Muslim but despises the extremists who defile the Koran. And he doesn't have hard feelings toward his family for running out on him.

· · · · · · · ·

Old Man Cornbread is about 65, and has been here 29 years. He has no one, no family that cares enough to send a mere post card. He loves to walk. The shoes the state furnishes are canvas slip-ons (cheap China-made) and wear out quickly; if you walk as much as Ol' Cornbread does they are trash even quicker. To get another pair is such a hassle. We bought a used pair of tennis shoes for $7.00 and after I cleaned them up and traded a dollar for a pair of insoles for them, we gave them to Ol' Man Cornbread. When we gave them to him I thought he was going to cry. He put them on right then and it was like he was walking on air. He had a big smile all over his face and was bouncing with every step.

He doesn't talk much; he just walks around and he loves cornbread. He won't ask for extra cornbread or ask anyone for theirs if they're not going to eat it, but I always give him mine and gather up a couple pieces from others for him. He always says thanks. He's a good old man. It was a great feeling when we gave him the sneakers.

To see him zooming around during our floor time is kool. Once a week we get an hour and a half of outside yard time and his first time with his "new" sneakers was very kool. He was zooming and smiling; we did good. We make a great team. Happiness from helping people is a good kind of happy. I wish I could adequately describe it. You know, I'm sure you know the "look," the "happy look" I'm talking about; it shows when you've helped someone and they appreciate your help, especially someone who rarely receives any kindness and who is basically ignored in life like he doesn't matter. Well, we're showing some guys that some people do care about them.

Saving a Life

Much as I used to hate child molesters [chomos], one time the [guards] put one in with us. When I realized what was up, everything went deathly quiet. Psycho Mike and Hatchet Jack were getting their shanks off the top of the ductwork in the bathroom and I knew they were fixing to pop more holes than a sieve in this little geeky nerd-looking dude and slice him up, so I got off my bed and went straight at the dude. When I got in his face I said, "You sick chomo maggot piece of shit I'm gonna kill your m-f–ing ass," and slapped him, but cupped my hand right before it connected so it would pop loud and sound like I really hit him harder than what I did and said under my breath, "Run for the door or they're gonna kill you!" And he did just that. I acted like I tripped and couldn't grab him fast enough.

They locked me up for assault but I didn't care because those two killers would have killed him. As much as I hated child molesters, I still didn't want him to die. I even looked proper in the other inmates' eyes because I attacked a chomo. The dude's Mom wrote to me and said her son told her what I did. I thought she was going to cuss me out for slapping her son, but she said, "My son said you saved his life." And he explained how I did it. She sent me $50 and a box full of novels. Ain't that something? The dude went to Protective Custody. I didn't want to harm the dude, but that was the only option I could see.

. . . .

We inmates have to stay on our guard because this place is so full of negativity. Prisoners need to be prepared mentally. We know a full-blown shakedown can jump off at any time where the guards are subject to confiscate any or everything. They can do pretty much whatever they want and we can't do much at all about it. We can either deal with it with a "Nuttin' 2it" mind frame, which is the smart way to deal with any situation you may encounter as a prisoner. Or, you can "go off," raising hell, screaming, yelling, banging on steel, or flooding the tier [with toilet/sink water]. If you just chill, remain calm and stay in control, you can deal with whatever they come at you with. If you "raise hell" you're doing exactly what they want! They don't give a damn how much hell you raise. They'll stand back until you're tired or just hit you with super-hot mace and throw you in the Hole.

. . . .

The guards I've seen change for the better aren't the sharpest as far as education goes, but they can read people real good. They read me and saw I was being straight with them and that's what I mean when I say you have to be real, you have to show others the kindness that is within. They have to see your smile in your eyes and words and deeds; they have to be able to feel the Koolness of Buddha's teaching, Bro. If I had been phony with the Buddha's teaching, that guard who helped me with the Sacks of Kindness sure wouldn't have been working up a sweat running up and down three tiers delivering Sacks of Kindness with a smile in his eyes. When folks see and feel you're for real, they respond in a more positive way about Buddhism.

....

Mindfulness and attentiveness need to stay fresh in an inmate's mind. I've had a wrecking crew of guards rush my cell in the middle of the night, snatch everything, all my property, every piece of paper, soap, cup, everything, and leave me with the pair of boxers I was wearing and one blanket, the whole time yelling in my face, telling me to give up the knife they knew I had, had just got it, they knew I had it, we'll find it, blah, blah and before they left said, "You just thought you was gonna stick the Captain!" The Captain was pissed off, but not at me! He was mad at the guards because they were in the wrong blocks. They weren't even supposed to be bothering me! The Captain made them apologize, put my stuff back in order and pay me for a new radio because they broke mine in their overzealousness. Actually one guard stomped it, but, once again, I let the dude slide even though the Captain knew it didn't get busted up like that by being dropped. He was glad I didn't press the issue and so was the guard. We actually got kind of Kool after that. But, had I reacted, went off raising hell, it would have quickly escalated and the situation would have been out of control, possibly with one or two of them and me getting hurt. I just stayed calm and exercised patience. You have to stay in a Mindful mode. I tell these guys to stay in control. Some listen, most don't.

....

Every time I talk to him [a particular guard] I see that scar right below his eye and think how close he came to being blinded by a kid confused by hate and anger and endless other problems. The real confusing part is my friend isn't one of the self-righteous assholes totally consumed by anger and hate. He will go out of his way to help someone, black or white. This is a madhouse,

Bro, where death or disfigurement and violence are only a heartbeat away. What better place for me to spread Loving-kindness?

. . . .

When you really want to help the guards in here, responding to them, no matter what, with kindness and calmness and humbleness, when you know you've done nothing wrong and they're just in unskillful mode/ignorant mode/childish mode, meet them with kindness and understanding. If you react to them in any other way, the negative karma is then also in your pocket. Take, for example, when I didn't go "burning" that big Ol' Bruiser/Brawler/Hateful Medea/racist guard. It matters to me that I respond, that I act skillfully. They'll never change to being a kind and compassionate being if you act unskillfully! You have to show them by being a Buddha in all your thoughts and actions.

I might be the only encounter with Buddha's teachings that someone has in his life, so I need to properly represent Buddha with my character, behavior, and actions. I must be Mindful that hate is only overcome with love, not more hate or anger.

. . . .

I am back here [in the Hole] for a noble reason (I think). I was being escorted by two police guards when a cricket was trying to get across the hall. With the stormy, rainy day, the bugs and critters are stirring around in prison. The guard on my right, a troubled, very unhappy hateful individual was going to stomp on this cricket. No way in hell was that going down. I shouldered his cruel ass against the wall and said, "What the f– is wrong with you, trying to stomp that cricket? How'd you like it if a Big sonbitch stomped on you?" I almost got my ass kicked but it would've been worth it.

I just found the [Buddhist] Precept for saving my little cricket friend's life: "Should you see a worldly person intent on killing an animal, attempt by 'appropriate means' to rescue or protect it and to free it from its misery." That guard was intent on killing my Little Critter friend so I used appropriate means.

Yes, I am proudly doing thirty days in the Hole for saving the life of a friend. Bro, their beautiful music has helped me de-stress and get centered many more times than I can count. They've appeared in my cell at times when I'm completely off balance and not in control, as if they sensed I needed help and when their beautiful music fills my cell. In just a few minutes of meditation with their music softly playing, I'm okay again. Their music is so spiritual, Bro. Next time you're out hiking and chilling in the woods, listen for them; close your eyes and let their music speak to your heart. Listen with your ears and your Heart and you'll "feel" what I'm talking about.

The physical suffering I'm experiencing now in the Hole is worth it to me. I'd do it again Bro, even if I had to go through this sickness and ill health again, I would. There is No Koolness in killing.

Bro, if I could have just picked up my little Cricket Friend to save his life I would have. Not only would the cruel young guard have stopped me, he then would have stomped my little friend and I'd have had no chance to save him. It takes me a bit to bend or squat to pick up something off the floor and I was in cuffs and waist chain. The "old school" guard would have allowed it but not the young one. Had you seen the look on his face of pure evil, a cruel gleam in his eyes and face, you would realize I took the only action possible to save my Friend.

I've apologized to the guard but to no avail. He wants to beat me down so bad, and really, I don't care if he does. Like I said before, any suffering I encounter because of what I did is no big deal. There ain't any beating they can give me that will compare to what I experienced from my own father. So be it.

. . . .

You understand the beautiful music of animals, Bro. Your frogs and birds in Eugene speak to your heart. It's beyond words, huh? Oh you'll love this. The night before last, I woke up to a cricket singing away in my cell! It was so awesome. For about an hour he just played the sweetest tune. I cried some joyful tears my friend and I just know it was a "thank you" concert for saving my little Friend a few months ago. Talk about a smile in my heart! He left and went down the tier, stopping every so often to play some sweet music, then moved on. Very Kool! There's joy everywhere!

PART II
PARTNERS

CHAPTER 6

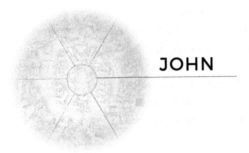

JOHN

Roy

The first time I met John I was just getting out of the Hole after five consecutive months. I was still in self-destruct mode because I hadn't been turned on to Buddha's teachings yet. I just couldn't see even trying to do the fresh Life Without Parole/Slow Death Sentence. When I bumped into John he asked, "Bro', you okay? Need some help?" He didn't even know me, but instead of being a regular asshole hardass (he outweighed me by 60 lbs. and was muscled up), he was looking and listening for a way to help somebody. He said, "I know who you are and what you're charged with and I know a lot of shit happened in your life to cause shit to get you here. " He said, "Folks don't want to hear about crazy shit. I got your back and will help you get back in shape. Don't give up. Don't let the system win."

John and I just fit together like good Biker Bros of the world. We are a great team and he would fight to the death to help protect me from harm. He's the brother I never had.

John

I was born in the summer of 1965 on the south side of Chicago to child-molesting parents, aunts, uncles, and cousins. My family bloodline consists of Sicilian, Moor, and Native Indian. I was an outcast at birth. I was the fifth child but a half [brother] to three older sisters and half [brother] to one older brother. Not only did our parents molest us and force us upon each other, but mentally and physically we were abused. They forced us to drink alcohol and do drugs, just to see the effects. All my siblings were beaten and thrown in the basement starting at age three. By the time I was three we had moved from Chicago to Arkansas and on to Indiana.

My first experience of being scared shitless was at the age of three. I had refused to eat my beets and my mother threw me outside on the porch all night. I fell asleep from exhaustion, crying and beating upon the screen door, swearing I'd never be bad again. In the morning I was awakened by being yanked off the porch by my hair and thrown in the basement after a fierce beating. I came to love the basement because I found my insect and amphibian friends a comfort.

Now let me explain what a beating was. Beatings consisted of using thick leather belts, belt buckles, razor straps, fists, feet, extension cords, hoses, 2x4 studs, or six foot long rowing oars. Basically, whatever was on hand. The beatings stopped when they got tired of beating you or you lay bleeding and unconscious. Back then nobody got involved with the person next door's problems. Several times we were rushed to the emergency room with critical "accidents." The doctor sometimes would ask how it happened. When my mother would begin to tell the doctors, the doctors would tell her to be quiet because they wanted to hear it from us. We knew better than to say anything. The beatings and the basement were our doom so we would say we had an accident. Then we would move to another state for a while.

We grew up with no friends because we weren't allowed to have any, which is why I have no societal communication. I was the youngest and a half-brother, so I was an outcast to my siblings. Instead, nature became my friend. Love was something we were taught to think of as an emotion, and emotions were taught as a weakness. There was no such thing as Santa Claus. We starved a lot. My father was gone a lot on a truck or stayed away from home. When he was home, he was drunk or high or both, which resulted in bad things happening. By the time I was six, I was an alcoholic, loved drugs, smoked cigarettes, and was adept at having sex with both males and females.

I've got to talk about my father killing our pets. He made us raise them, and would THEN make us kill them. Even though it doesn't sound like much, it's part of what caused us kids to grow up with no conscience. We were already taught there was no such thing as love and to have no emotions such as fear or happiness. These in combination alone made me a cold-hearted child. Believe it or not, it still haunts me to this day. Now this is where it gets tricky to explain with what I was taught as a child, which is basically that you can "care" for something and still kill it.

To explain: Even though I now care for life and know the meaning of life, it will never erase the no-conscience ability within me. If it came down to it I could kill, even though I might not like it. It would not faze [sic] me in the least. If I was a [mercenary], I would be perfect for the job. As a civilian it is a terrible trait, yet it's something that no one should have. Sad to say, there are many people like me on this planet where their youth was stolen from them from birth. Some lived on the streets as children, or because of war or disease and famine. This is how your tyrants are formed, so yes, it seems that one thing my father did was lesser, but it is much more.

Bad to Worse

In 1975 we moved from Bryan, Ohio to the middle of Louisiana. That's when I found out what racism was for the black inside of me—the Moor—and what a Yankee was. For one year I fought "coon asses" one, two, and three at a time. Lucky for me that my father and mother taught us boxing, street fighting, martial arts, the use of knives, guns, and homemade bombs. My father was gone one whole year, so we didn't have friends. But you'd be surprised at how church people love well-endowed little boys, [and I was molested by both men and women from church]. [The church] supplied us with eggs, chicken meat, and cases of pork bones from the butcher and his "loving" wife.

We (my one remaining older sister and me, as my brother had left) got so malnourished that our teeth turned yellow, which affects me to this day. All our hair fell out and we defecated worms. We were called the mangy Yankees.

Then in 1976 my dad showed up in the middle of the night, packed us up, and moved us to a swampy area in Texas, population thirty-two. I was eleven years old then and that's when my life became a living hell. My sister got pregnant at 15 years old in order to get out of the house and my brother had joined the Marines. I became the one who took all the blame, hate, sex, and punishment. That's when my father became a religious fanatic and I became a hater of God. All the old stuff still happened. I still had sex with all kinds of grown-ups, even within the church.

I became a waif upon the streets of Houston in 1977. The event that led to living on the streets began when an ex-Vet came one day to borrow my father's tools to fix his tractor. My pregnant mother was away in town when the man found me tied by my hands, hanging from the barn rafters as my father was beating me with a horse bridle. My father got his clock cleaned thoroughly by that Vet and before passing out I remember trying to smile through swollen, bloody lips.

When I awoke, the Vet and his wife were beside me—they had taken me in. I found out that he had told my father that he didn't deserve kids and if he ever touched me again he'd kill him. His two sons became my best friends for the three months it took me to heal. During that time I stole money from the surrounding community, including the church's offering plate. Then I packed a small duffel bag and ran away.

My true learning of survival came when Deborah and Ermine found me digging in the dumpster behind the strip joint where they worked. These two saviors took me off the street, clothed and fed me, and gave me a place to live. They also taught me the code of the streets. They taught me how to use my body to survive by turning tricks with single people, married people, and groups. All were white. Lawyers, doctors, police, judges, secretaries, drug dealers, gun runners, bikers—all were the same, and there was no difference between followers of the law and criminals. I hated them all.

At 14 years old, I was riding freight trains across the country, knew drugs, and had seen death in many forms. I was a menace to society. I had a .357 Magnum with special tips that had been outlawed by the federal government. I robbed people and stores and stole cars. Robbing drug pushers was fun and easy; I'd walk up, pull the gun, and shoot them in the leg and take their money and dope. Before I turned 17 and went to jail, I had been from coast to coast, border to border, and lived a life of sex, drugs, alcohol, violence, and unspeakable crime.

At 16 years old I stole a car from Beaumont, Texas, and was caught twenty-two hours later, eight miles from the California border on Interstate 8 going to San Diego. It was 1982 and I had a 1982 Firebird. I went to Yuma, Arizona Juvenile Detention Center where I fought extradition to Texas. Twenty-eight days later they came to get me. Had it been two more days I'd have been free, but destiny did not have that in my future.

When I got to Texas, the man whose car I stole never pressed charges, but the State picked up the charges because I had one hell of a juvenile record. They charged me with unauthorized use of a vehicle and sentenced me to three years in the Texas Department of Corrections. They held me until I turned 17 and then charged me with a misdemeanor. At that age I had one hell of a lesson because they had put me in one of the five roughest prisons in Texas. Women didn't even work in them in 1982. Grown men were getting raped then.

In 1983 I had "Destroyer" tattooed on my chest. In those days when you entered prison you had only two choices: F– or Fight. Either one could kill you. Kill or be killed—physically, mentally, and spiritually. People were crazy and would cut on themselves or commit suicide to get out of it. Now-a-days it's not as extreme. From time to time you have rapes, killings, stabbings, and fights but if you're smart you stay in shape and always keep eyes in all directions. And it's not because of what you may have done; it could be because of something a friend of yours did. Something you may know nothing about. A guard could not like you and pay an inmate to do something to you.

While in prison I saw the most evil and vile acts humans could do to one another. I saw stabbings, and killings, and suicides. People were burned and thrown off the Third Tier. I saw heads cut off and people beaten to death. I became hard, vicious, and cold-blooded. I learned crime from the best in there.

········

Even as bad as I was in the world, I helped people when I could. I gave time to children and helped with special people. Why? Because they had no one to defend them, and I had seen too much abuse in my life as a child to have people hurt or mistreated. In fact, one time I helped an elderly couple in Bayan, Ohio. There were two brothers in their 20s who had just gotten out of prison and they started harassing the elderly in the trailer park they lived in. I knew one of the older guys when I was a child. Well, I went to their trailer one night (I was intoxicated), and whooped both of them. I got two assault charges, was fired from my job. It caused a divorce to my second wife. Was it worth it? Yes. Those two never messed with the elderly again. Not while I was there.

········

One day I met a man who was a U.S. Special Forces Vietnam Veteran. His name was Wallace and he had done four tours. This man had seen his share of bloodbaths and had done his share. Mentally, he was screwed up when he came out of Nam. When I met him he was still going to a psychiatrist.

To know him you would never have guessed that he had problems. He started teaching me how to turn my anger at the world off and go to positive thinking. He related to me like no other had. I was skeptical at first out of old habits. I watched him around others. He would come to get me when he was going to town or somewhere else. He always looked for the best in everyone, but he passed on in 2001 from a massive heart attack. I lost the best friend I ever had in life.

. . . .

I realized that Wallace had given me the gift of seeing the good in people. He gave me patience. The other seeds showed me the good inside me. There were inmates that would bless me with a soup, some coffee, weed, or dope. These were people who didn't even know who I was. They were just people I was on the hoe squad with.

I had no family or friends. All I had was one friend and she was in her mid-sixties when we had started writing. She said her faith in God impressed it upon her heart. I wasn't too sure about God. I knew he existed, but I knew he didn't have anything to do with me. Heck, I cussed him. Oh how wrong I was. I now have faith. I am not religious. I am not a Christian. I have faith.

. . . .

I miss my wife. All three of them! Seriously, though, I miss the walks, the cuddling, watching TV, movies, and sitting on the porch swing watching storms. I miss the long drives across the country just sightseeing. I miss having someone and not feeling alone and lonely.

"The Black Timber Wolf"

I lost the best friend I ever had in life [when Wallace died]. Slowly I turned back to the evil ways. I was married then and had just had a daughter in 1998. I felt something I had never felt before; it made me have a funny feeling inside that actually scared me. It was a feeling "above caring." Over two and a half years I fell in love with [my daughter].

> *When John's daughter was around two-and-a-half, he learned that his brother had been molesting her.*

I went to the law for help … No go. So I left my little family because I knew what I had to do; I had to become detached emotionally from them. I allowed what I call the black timber wolf loose. When it comes out I cannot control him until he is done with his bloodlust. It sounds like a psychopath or socio-path, right? Well, I was seeing a psychiatrist and drawing a mental health check from the U.S. Government. I traded my prescribed drugs for illicit drugs and went back to alcohol and evil ways ten times worse than before.

In May of 2002 John, while drunk and high, took a shotgun and went with his nephew to the home of his brother and sister-in-law, who was pregnant.

My nephew was with me for the slaughter of this man and his family. Then it was over. My black timber wolf went back into his lair.

. . . .

I have committed a lot of crimes, from childhood to adulthood. Now I am in prison with three LWOs [three life without parole sentences, one each for his brother, his sister-in-law, and their unborn baby]. I have, in my heart, asked all for forgiveness and I have forgiven myself. Yet, do I suffer because I am still in prison? Why should I feel suffering for something I have done to myself? They didn't do it, I did. You know what I do sometimes? I sit back and listen to all the BS going on outside my cell and I study my cell walls, everything within, including my white clothing and then I look at the cell bar door. I put within my mind: "You will most likely die here, you know that? There's probably a one in one trillion chance that you will get out, but it's not probable." Do you know what the next action is? I start laughing so hard that tears come to my eyes. It's because I think how smart I was to show the world I was tough and I was going to make something of myself. Boy, I showed them! Didn't that take intelligence? Oh, there are days that I get frustrated. It's not from being incarcerated though. It's because I now have so much to give and can't. I have learned so much and this is my price—not suffering.

CHAPTER 7

INTO THE MIND

John

Complex mind games are played in here, but I sit inside my cell and I look out at the Dayroom floor. Sometimes it's full of people; other times everybody is in their cells. There are 54 cells. I can see 44 of them. I sit and listen to conversations, and watch their actions and I laugh so hard because it's the same games I've seen [doing] 30 years hard. The results are always the same, just different players. Even the world outside this fence has a routine that does not change.

When I sit on my concrete bunk and look out my armor-plated window, I see the inside compound and the triple fence, one being 5,000 volts at 243 mega-amps. I feel the hot and cold of the block wall made of inner and outer brick. The rover truck passes by every 11½ minutes. I can see a guard tower; at night it's supposed to do a searchlight check every thirty minutes. At night the compound is lit up with powerful night lights.

Where I am now, I face north. Over the tops of the fences lies a stretch of land divided into separate fields. I see this because I'm on the second tier and there are three tiers all together. Half a mile away the inmates are lined up and chopping the ditches.

The inmates of course are all in white. The guards wear blue and ride horses. They used to carry .357 Magnums with 55 grain .38 bullets. Now they all carry powerful Glocks with three extra magazines. A high rider is in the woods with his 30.06 [rifle] just in case someone decides to run. There are five guards called hoe riders and one acting lieutenant. Then there's the officer in the truck with a Remington shotgun and a Glock. So a runner would first have to outrun one hundred and five 40-caliber bullets and fifteen .223 bullets and four No. 8 steel shot, ¾ inch nitromag .12 gauge bullets.

The woods come in spurts. There is a rotating aluminum water duct pipe that waters the field and is 240 feet long and twelve feet off the ground. The sky above me is clear, yet it lacks the vibrant blue of the Northwestern sky. It looks as if it has been watered down ninety percent. I see the heat waves dancing in the distance.

A plane is flying over, spraying the fertilizer and maybe insecticide. Yet I feel none of it. I can't touch any of it. I can't smell any of it. I am thankful I can see it. I am thankful I am still here to appreciate the miracle that "I" am and all that is about me. Civilizations have been and will be. Another will be gone again. It's always a birth of a new beginning. Every second is a new beginning.

During his time in prison, John has served more than 270 days in solitary confinement as punishment for masturbation in front of prison employees, which is a violation of Arkansas Department of Correction rules.

Sexuality is like a bonfire that flares up. People say, "I can't imagine how this came about. It just erupted." But in fact all along we have been gathering and piling up the wood. Bringing the gasoline and pouring it on. Then carefully we take out the match, strike it, and throw it on the pile.

[My stint in solitary] started after I was accidentally accused [of masturbating in front of an officer]. The woman guard wrote down the wrong cell number while picking up dinner trays one day. When she got back to the control booth later, she wrote the disciplinary [report] for the cell she remembered. She had the next day off, and I got a disciplinary with six different charges on it. The next day I went to court and I was found guilty. Even though I showed them in all those years incarcerated up to that point (8 years), I had never ever had any charges that even remotely were related to that. All I ever had was dirty urine, green money, dope, and refusing to work.

Well, the third day following she was back to work. I asked her why she lied and wrote me this bogus disciplinary. She said she made a mistake and wrote the wrong cell number. I said, "No shit." I told her she had to tell them so I could get that off me, because with a charge like that I was going to be shut out of a lot of jobs. She told me no, because they'd fire her for falsification of documents. I told her it was a mistake but she was adamant. So I said, "You want to accuse me of something I didn't do, well I'll give you something to accuse me of." From November 2006 until now, I have masturbated [in front of] more than a hundred women. Only nine of those have written me up.

The reason is that it went from a revenge to an addiction. Because I have no chance to make it back to the world to have sex. All I have is my sexual fantasies. These women allow me to enjoy my sexual fantasies. I have some come to my cell and tell me to pull it out, let them see it. Others want to watch me have an orgasm. Others like to watch, but not get caught. Others like to be talked to nasty while you're doing it. Some play with themselves under the right circumstances. Others love when men masturbate on their ass in tight pants. This is not only guards, but employees of the Arkansas Department of Corrections and even nurses … that allow it, and watch it, and some of those come to the cell and ask to see it. And a person as myself—with sexual compulsion disorder—it is great and it is bad.

So one must see it is not only one way. Both men and women enjoy these fantasies because they cannot do it in the world. I keep on trying to quit though. My longest bid was 15 months. Now I'm back in lockdown for 16 months. Ha-Ha-Ha.

. . . .

I come back [to the Hole] of my own accord. Being in the Hole takes the pleasures of the carnal away and takes my mind off my mental track. I can sit here and listen to other inmates' misery and think how lucky I am that I have not let my mind slip that far. How sad it is that people are brought so low as human beings by other human beings.

There is no air conditioner or heater. For me, suffering is good for the soul. It also shows me and the police that they cannot win; even though they have to put me back here when I go against their rules, they know it does not bother me. I am still my same happy-go-lucky self. My body belongs to Mother Gaia, my soul to God. My thoughts are mine. What does that leave them? Here I have 30 days to purify my mind and body.

"I'm Alive Within"

The year was 1985. The month of March. I was in the Clark County Detention Center in Las Vegas. While I was there I met a man whose alias was "Holy Ghost." I never knew his real name. He was originally from Portland, Oregon. He loved doing armed robberies of jewelry stores. He got busted in Las Vegas while robbing one. He was sentenced to 45 years in Gene Penitentiary on Interstate 15 north of Vegas.

He was a Kung Fu teacher. He was teaching me Kung Fu when we were out of our cells. He taught me how to meditate. He taught me to get into the most relaxed position (without falling asleep), close your eyes and picture a white beam coming from the darkest of space. At the end of the white beam is a small orb. Take all your thoughts and throw them into this orb and it will suck up all your thoughts. Continue to do this until your mind is void of all thoughts. When you get to that level, you will feel like you are floating in water except you have no external feeling. When you master this and can control it, you then put a picture of something in your mind. I was told to start out with a simple rose. Then continue to build off the Rose. The Colors. Maybe dew dripping from it. Thorn or thornless. Etc. Until you have a whole landscape of whatever you desire. It brings such peace.

. . . .

[The best time to meditate] is when you are hyped out, angry, or depressed. These are the times we must become more mindful to be able to control our minds and our bodies. If you can't control them, how can your spirit become enlightened? I must assert myself deeper into controlling my mind and if I can't control it, how can I hope to be a benefactor in the community?

. . . .

First you must learn to master your own thoughts in order to make your body do what you want it to do. Until I learned this, I was a marionette and my strings were being pulled by untrained thoughts. Unharnessed thoughts caused me to do ignorant things. So even though I thought I was trying my hardest, I wasn't. I was only doing what I knew by repetition. Poke your finger in a wasp's nest and you are going to get stung every time.

. . . .

Another issue is being weak-minded; we are all guilty of this. For example, in here one inmate jumps up the cell door and calls another inmate a no-good… for no other reason than he doesn't like the way he looks. Now it's up to the other person to show where his mind is. Is it strong or weak? If he jumps out there and starts cussing and threatening back, he is weak-minded because he has allowed the other man's actions to penetrate his thoughts and cause him to do things that are totally against who he is. He lets the other man dictate his actions. He is then no longer in control of his own thoughts or actions.

. . . .

I am having fun back here [in the Hole] this time. Much more than ever before. I have a black square card about 6 in. by 5 in. In the center is a big yellow ball with a smiley face and looks like the face for Wal-Mart. On top it states: "I'm alive within." At the bottom it asks: "Are you?" Whenever I start having negative emotions I stand in front of it and stare into the unblinking black glossy eyes. I slow my breathing and at the same time analyze why I am starting to feel what I feel. Every time, that unwavering smile and honest stare gets me to laughing. I think everyone should have one. After a while that little yellow ball is ingrained permanently in your mind. It truly works.

. . . .

I have messed up my vow of silence. I began when the Asst. Warden came through passing out trays of food and Kool-aid and milk and yelled at me when I pointed at the sign I had made: "Milk/juice, one of each." He was cussing, but I gave him the benefit of the doubt and in sign language said, "I cannot speak." He said I was holding him up, so I pointed to the porter who told him about my vow of silence. He then got to saying some foul stuff and my temper started to rise as he was disrespecting and violating my religious belief. After two minutes he slammed the door and everyone in isolation heard what he had said to me. The porter was looking at me, knowing I wanted to jump out and smack and cuss the Asst. Warden, but I kept my cool. I ate my supper, washed my tray, and put it in the trap, then sat down and started reading the Metta Sutta. I heard the food cart coming around and the door opened and it was a sergeant, a woman who never speaks to me. She said, "I heard what your uncle told you." I looked at her and said, "Don't ever call that man my uncle." The porter, who is also a Buddhist, said, "There went that vow." I felt so bad that I apologized to the sergeant then sat down and meditated.

The Gift of Caring

Just as I had done with Roy, I sent small amounts of money to John so he could spread kindness to other inmates with food and other items from the commissary.

The look on people's faces when they are blessed [with an act of kindness] out of the blue is worth all the gold in the world. I've thought of all the evil I've committed. I've thought of all the energy I put into it. Why couldn't I take that same energy, harness it, and apply it to helping others? This is a special gift, because when a person believes no one cares, he gives up on life. We as humans must have affection and love. We must know that someone out there truly cares.

· · · · · · · ·

A porter came to me and told me a friend of mine was in the Hole. Now, I've known him for eleven years and seen him go to the Hole three times. He's got a 30-year sentence. In the Hole, as you know from my letters, you can't take food, books, radio, etc. But you can take your 6-ounce coffee cups for drinking water, juice, milk, coffee, or Kool-Aid. He sent me a request for a coffee cup, so four days later I bought two brand new ones and sent them by a sergeant. It wasn't much—86 cents each—but out of all his "friends," I was the only one that would help him. That made me feel good.

· · · · · · · ·

Here's how I helped others. Some people needed envelopes. Most I helped out by giving out soups, chips, candy, cakes, crackers, and stuff they don't get because they have no one. With each of them I let them know that they were blessed because I was blessed and that I do not look for anything in return, only that they help another. No matter how small or petty the act may seem, it plants a seed of care in that person's mind. No matter if that person turns completely destructive, that memory of kindness will always be there.

· · · · · · · ·

I paid off small debts for three people to keep them from serious trouble; one was $12.00, one $10.00, and another $6.00. Many people think I'm crazy for helping other people. They say, "Why do you give your commissary to others when you're out? You don't get no help from them." They don't understand that when you help others, no matter whether they return it to you or not, it is the fact that you as a human being are doing your part in life to construct a new and better social structure for the present that will carry over into the future. It does not matter what color, creed, enslaved, or free person you or they are, for we are all enslaved to one thing or another, whether mentally, physically, spiritually, or emotionally. It's what you do in your enslavement with what you have that loosens the bonds that hold you.

· · · · · · · ·

Out of love and respect, I take time to listen. Here in solitary there is a 21-year-old black guy who everyone picks on. I am the only one who will talk to him. The others ask me why I mess with the dude. I tell them that just because they don't like him, they should not expect me not to like him. This is why everyone gets along with me—inmates and guards alike. I don't change. I treat everyone the same no matter who they are. I don't see color or crime. I listen or if needed, give my thoughts to their problems. In turn I have learned about myself. I am content. I have reached a level of awareness that I feel others' emotions when I look at them, or, by their speech. I can tell their whole life by their eyes and actions. It's a gift I once hated and I now love.

Out of 467 inmates here now, Roy and I know at least 430 of them. They know both of us and know our compassion and kindness and that we are studying Buddhism. We are trusted and respected. Some fear us, which I wish they didn't, but from our past lives this fear exists. We still carry that heavy weight thinking in many people's minds—we were once considered badasses. They know you don't lose that. They don't know you can master it.

CHAPTER 8

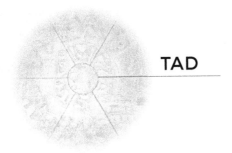

TAD

Name: Roger "Tad" Price, Jr.

Date of Birth: Aug. 13, 1979

Education: GED

Family: Never married, one son

Prison time: Sentenced in 2002 to 15 years in prison for rape. Previously served 2 years for various crimes.

Roy

I met Tad here in Barracks No. 6. He was above me. I was listening to the outside chatter while reading dharma material and writing letters, etc. I was listening to see if I would pick up on somebody needing help of some kind. I found out that Tad was trying to find art supplies to draw something for some guy. I got to listening in more closely and he was getting down with some real Bodhisattva soldiering by fixing radios for a couple of soups but he didn't ask for anything. He gave away soups and coffee and helped guys who had nothing and nobody and were without hustle—people skills. He helped all, including black, white, Mexican, no matter as anyone needing help he'd tell them "No problem." I started looking out for him while he was looking out for others.

He drew kool dharma stuff. I shared dharma material with him and he told me he didn't believe it's all over when you die and I said, "Not over by a long shot." He liked my happy-go-lucky motto, "Nuttin' 2it." I started using my connections to make sure he got plenty of art materials and radio repair stuff because I saw he wasn't asking for money in return for what he did and I knew many guys who have no help. When someone offered to pay him, he accepted, but always undercharged. We made a good Bodhisattva team. With some special materials he made beautiful Mother's Day cards that would have sold easily but Tad didn't charge because he said all Moms are special even if the son is an asshole, so all Moms deserve love. He made a lot of Moms happy two years ago and I'm positive he will do it every year. He's an impressive, good-hearted person doing whatever and whenever, for whomever to make the world a better place.

Tad

Roy and I, we share childhoods that shouldn't have been. He let his [pain and anger] out by ending lives. Me, I tried taking my own life when I was 16 years old. I'll start after my attempted suicide. I tried to kill myself with a .38 gun because I just wanted the pain and hatred to end (because of my childhood). I put the pistol to my head and pulled the trigger: nothing but a click. As I was putting the gun down, my older brother walked into the dining room. He asked what I was doing so I lied. When he left, I opened the bullet changer and saw where the firing pin hit dead center, but the bullet hadn't fired. I saved that bullet for years.

Then a girl named Lisa came back into my life. That was about three years before prison. She was my first love when we were kids. She moved and came back years later and was about 14 or 15 at the time and I was about 17 years old. Her father and my stepdad had a racetrack, so Lisa and I saw each other a lot. It took me a while to work up the nerve to tell her how I always had felt about her.

Now Lisa had a little girl named Anna who she had when she was 13 years old. I didn't care because I just wanted her back into my life, but there was one problem. I didn't want her to find out about my childhood because I knew she wouldn't want to be in my life. So we moved into a house together with her little girl. She was pregnant at this time with my son. But I must say this. Before we moved into our own house, I was accepted in Texas for a scholarship to the University of Houston. My grandmother had helped me obtain it and I planned to set up everything in Texas, then come back to get Lisa and Anna. Lisa told me that if I left and went to Texas, she would get an abortion. So I didn't leave; I let that scholarship slip away. I just recently told my grandmother the truth about the choice I was given: education or my son.

Lisa and I moved into our own house to get away from our families. I also thought it would protect her from the truth of my childhood. Things were going great; when my son was born I was proud and every moment of that day in the hospital is implanted in my mind; it was the first real joy I ever found in life. I loved Lisa and Anna and my son.

Then I started working for my landlord, on weekends. When she came onto me really hard I turned her down, then she sued me and said I had broken the front door and cut down a tree in the yard. We moved into another house, which was really nicer, but I never told Lisa why we moved. In this house, I also worked for the owner in my spare time. Soon I was working two or three jobs, trying to pay the bills. I was doing my part as a father and husband.

Then all went downhill fast. Lisa started letting my so-called friend John be at my house when I was out of town working. Yes, she was cheating on me. Twice I told her to leave and live with her dad. The third time I caught her cheating she tried to kill my son; she had put a knife to his neck. But my love for her kept me with her; still, I couldn't forgive her for cheating on me when I was working. The sad part is that she always accused me of cheating, but the truth is I couldn't do it. By this time I was torn up inside and all that pain and hatred came back and more.

It got to the point that all I wanted to do was stay drunk because I just didn't care anymore. I purposefully lost everything and we went from living in a house to living with a family member. All I did was work construction in the day and work at KFC at night. I told my mom everything and she said, "Just leave." So that is what I was going to do. I took the kids for a walk and tried to explain to them but they knew something was wrong because the hurt and tears said everything.

The day I had planned on leaving is when I was accused of raping my family member's stepdaughter, who said I had tied her to her bed and taped her mouth shut. I had planned to meet a girl from work and stay at her house and leave for Texas the next morning.

One day I would like to tell the truth to Lisa. Let her know everything about my childhood and why I shut down on her, went numb to the point that the sight of her disgusted me. I still loved her and would easily sacrifice my life for hers. But no pain can compare to the last time I saw the kids. That day holds me to the bones. The jailors had to come and pull them from the bars because they wouldn't let go.

Lisa came to see me and had the nerve to say she was sorry and that "things were not supposed to go this far." When she said that, I knew then she had something to do with that girl's story of how I was supposed to have raped her. It made sense because that was one of Lisa's lies to cover up how she got pregnant with Anna at age 12 years old.

By this time I didn't give a damn about anything or anyone. Hate was all I knew. Pain was going to give out from that moment on. For years I blamed myself for her behavior, telling myself, "If I hadn't worked so much …" My mom said it was not my fault because I was only doing what a real man would do, and that was providing for my family. There is so much truth that needs to come out and one day I hope it does because I would sure like to get together with Lisa and the kids and a couple of others, especially with the girl I was supposed to have raped.

A Different Path

Tad had already served about eight years of his sentence when he met Roy. He'd developed an interest in Eastern religion and was studying Hinduism, but Roy introduced him to Buddhism, suggesting it was something "more worth [his] time." They studied together for about six months before Tad was transferred to a different prison, the Cummins Unit in Grady, Arkansas.

Kindness didn't develop in my life; it saved my life. And that's why Roy and I became so close. We share childhoods that shouldn't have been.

Roy gave me a book, one that you sent him while at the Max. I didn't get around to reading it until I was at Cummins. It's *The Art of Sitting* by John Daido Loori. This [horoscope] was hidden within the pages. Roy cut it out and placed it in there, knowing I would find it: "Leo (July 23–Aug. 22) Don't wait until you're satisfied with all the uncertainties to present your project to the world. That day will never come. There always will be unanswered questions. That's why you need partners."

I'm a Leo and this is how close Roy and I were spiritually. There are things that happened while we were in the barracks together that no one else would believe, so we share them in secret. That only proves to me that he and I were meant to meet, just like you [Doug] and I.

At Cummins, Tad met Tran, a prisoner who had previously trained as a Buddhist monk. Tran would talk with Tad about Buddhist texts, books, meditation, and his correspondence with me.

For hours I would sit and talk to him. Several people told me to feel honored because he doesn't talk. So, I asked him why he chose to talk to me. He said, "Your will is strong and destined for greatness. But the hate you have deep inside stops you." I asked him how he knew this. He stated, "My master trained me to see people." Then he walked me through how to overcome past hate. He said, "Now you see it. Now you don't." (My stepfather was the root of my past pain and hate.) This guy showed me a new way to look at my past, one that was complicated yet simple. He said, "Love, yet don't see that person for who he was. Just know now, how you are."

You mentioned how you judge people sometimes. That is a blessing, yet a curse when perceived wrong. My advice when this happens is: stop and see their good habits or actions. Mindful practice and love at the same time.

· · · · · · · ·

Tran, the monk, told me that mindfulness is just "proper focus," being relaxed without emotion. Emotion is a weakness because you are not focused. He asked me, "What do you know of meditation and mindfulness?" I said, "The books I've read." And he said, "Stop right there. Did you write that book?" I said, "No." Then he said, "That is not your path to enlightenment." He told me to forget everything I've read and start over. To search as you meditate to find your inner path. He said that true meditation is not hard, to just feel your breaths and relax. Then feel the energy outside your body and it would help you strengthen your sixth sense.

· · · · · · · ·

Pride is very thick in here, as Tran told me. He was trained in a cave not in a monastery, but he's now doing life in prison. He told me that "One should never try to change or direct a man; instead, allow your light to do it. Just walk beside them."

CHAPTER 9

THE PERFECT PLACE

Tad

One of the best places to practice compassion is in prison. Sad to say, but true. The definition of compassion as "pity" just doesn't fit for me. But in here, compassion is hard to show, and not accepted most of the time because to their way of thinking you are setting them up for a trick or "game" as they call it. But if one can get the practice down in here, people out there will think one is a God, so to speak.

. . . .

Once I learned [mindfulness] was really a focus training, I realized for years I've been doing it and never knew it. You see, one must always be mindful in here, including anything that requires movement around another inmate. Early in my beginning of doing time I witnessed a man being beaten because someone scuffed the guy's shoes by not watching where he was going. Then I saw a man get his throat cut because he stepped in front of another man; in here that is very disrespectful unless one says "Excuse me."

There is something called "soft eyes" that you may have heard of. In here, it is a must. Always pay attention to your surroundings. Always. Some of these guys will stab you for the fun of it or in order to get transferred.

Prison is a horrible place for anyone that has a conscience, but if one is trying to find a better way, this is the perfect place, because if one can master and channel this hate into positive energy, then out there nothing will faze him. His or her character is rooted in a better direction, one that, if it stays focused, will only continue to brighten into that "Guiding Light."

One thing I've learned about mindfulness is it helps you to appreciate the moment. I can't remember what book I read this in, but it said, "Each breath inhaled and exhaled is a new beginning." I like what you said about each moment being precious like water. Once upon a time I hated every moment in this place. Now I see each moment as a learning experience, one that will help mold me into a better person.

· · · · · · · ·

There is this new guy named Carp. He just moved into the barracks. I've been sharing your [writings on mindfulness] with him. We have become a team for mindfulness practice. He has become someone who understands my direction in life—to look at others as teachers. But he pointed out something I did not see: a lot of guys in this barracks look up to me. This did not affect my pride, but made me feel smaller, more humble. Strange.

· · · · · · · ·

I've been asked to assist in something that I consider a great honor. The Chaplain has allowed a couple of us into the chapel for one hour for meditation time. Yes! We are starting small, but some other inmates asked me to oversee the practice since I'm the only one they know with more experience. So, if you have any advice, please don't be afraid to help because I was really not expecting this. Yes, everything happens for a reason.

· · · · · · · ·

In my practice in here, I've noticed emotions are my weak point. There are so many uncalled for moments in prison when emotions run wild, if I let them. On days that I don't discipline myself I become "tense." When I'm being mindful there are "calm days" that pass by smoothly. Yes, less suffering and less stressful days is a great benefit to practicing mindfulness.

One thing [in] my practice is that when my emotions are high, my kindness is low.

Since the beginning of my practice I've never thought about mindfulness being upsetting. If we prevaricate (speak or act in an evasive way) on our path, then we miss the true meaning of practice; it's not for us and it never was. Yes, at first we realize a need, a hunger for something better. But, when wisdom sets in, mindfulness is not for us; it is for my spiritual side that sacrifices to serve others. We show compassion, kindness, good reasoning skills, etc. These are only the fruits of our practice. When I hold on to the feeling of appreciation or gratitude for an act, I miss the true meaning of "ethical living" because the self steps in and holds on to self. In vain living! Seeing these bad habits and correcting them mindfully brings an inner peace, sensual almost, because from my perspective I eliminate remorse and regret. "Pure actions" bring joy and happiness.

Living Through Art

Some of these guys ask me why I don't draw skulls and demons—prison stuff. I say there's enough ugly, negative energy in their world and when you have dealt with the amount of pain and hatred I have in life, you get to the point where you need some hope.

. . . .

When I draw, I now feel my work, not just see it, but become it—the way the pen or pencil feels in my hand, to the texture of the paper. Even smells catch my nose and each color has its own smell. No longer do I see myself as an artist, but one that creates. When people see my artwork or creation, they are now practicing being mindful. So—"creation of good practice." This practice has now built in me the habit of knowing that being mindful spreads more mindfulness.

. . . .

I didn't understand the purpose of my gift until a couple of years ago. It hit me that it was my legacy to bring smiles and beauty to the eyes of others. People thank me for the beautiful artwork, but in my head I'm telling them, "You made the opportunity possible." Guys in here ask for a soup or shot of coffee and say thank you, which is a sign of respect, and that's honorable. But that person has made the act of kindness and sacrifice possible. Now when I think back upon that old man's words about how this life is not ours to begin with, I smile.

. . . .

When I first began corresponding with Tad, I could see he was an artist. His earliest letters came in envelopes that had been decorated with elaborate patterns and bright colors—without access to paints and brushes, he used the crushed shells of candies like Skittles and M&Ms to create his pigments.

At first I thought the drawings were just abstract forms. But after receiving several letters, I realized that the envelopes were meant to be put together as a puzzle. A portion of his completed drawing, assembled from ten envelopes in two columns of five envelopes each, provides the cover art for this book.

My main point is the understanding deep within the artwork ... like my envelope puzzles. In today's modern age—cell phones, text, picture, internet—people don't really sacrifice the time, don't use personal mail anymore, and this [the envelope puzzle] brings that personal touch back with a little extra something that will grab people's attention....

. . . .

The deeper meaning in my art connects to the puzzle part. Life is a puzzle, an enigma, and we must search for the truth. I've studied different religions and noticed it is like a puzzle and when the pieces are put together properly, a beauty—truth—is seen. In my journey so far with Buddhism the pieces are coming together; when I see a Buddha sitting, I see a way of life, not just a man sitting.

The same applies to the roses I make. Roses are something man takes for granted, uses, and throws away, never seeing the sacrifice or the beauty. Whenever someone asks me to draw something for a family member or a friend, I ask questions such as "What do they like?" or "What's their favorite color?" because the drawing can only be made possible by them, for them. When an idea for a drawing comes to mind, it's because "a part of me" is showing forth. Everything has a greater meaning; it is up to us to search for it.

Although he had a strained relationship with other members of his family, for as long as he could remember, Tad's biggest champion, closest confidante, and strongest supporter had been his grandmother. In his youth, she had helped him get a scholarship, hoping he would attend college. After he was arrested, she paid for the best lawyer she could find to represent him. More recently, she had been making arrangements to have him come and live with her, and to help him get back on his feet once he was paroled in 2015.

Tad's grandmother had also been one of the few family members who kept in touch with him in prison, so when she stopped sending letters or taking his calls in 2014, he grew worried.

I found out what happened to my grandmother. It is not her health, but her own son. He has taken her phone from her and has 100% control of everything. His wife is the one that stole my grandmother's credit cards and checks and reduced her accounts to zero last year. My uncle hates the fact that I will be living with his mother because he knows I'm not going to put up with his crap. At this moment I feel useless. I can't do anything to help my grandmother. I can't even write her. Yes, he will intercept my mail, as he has done in the past. He and his wife are pill heads. Help me stay positive, my friend and partner. I need all the help I can at this moment. How do we disconnect from times like these when all we can do is sit back and watch those we love suffer from the hands of their own? I don't understand it. I try. I really do. Maybe one day all my practice will show through.

. . . .

If I was going to get out now, and I saw myself financially unable to keep up with the pressure, I would probably sell some drugs to make some "quick cash" to keep the parole officer happy. Now, the best part, let me tell you "how" my grandmother passed. My uncle was feeding her narcotics, heavy drugs, so he could get money from her. My sister told me he was getting $800–$1,000 dollars at a time from her, even after she was put in the nursing home. He would go up there. My sister told me that they knew about this for months but were too scared to do anything. That's why my sister is taking this so hard (guilt). Both of my uncles told my sister, if I get out and attempt anything, they are going to call my parole officer and have me sent back to prison. [My uncle's sister] told them that she had told me the truth of how they were treating her and how my grandmother's phone was disconnected by my uncle. He was also getting my mail and not letting my grandmother read it.

. . . .

For days I've been meditating, praying, even fasting—searching for guidance to handle my situation. So my sisters and I talked and flatting my time [serving out the prison sentence in its entirety, without taking parole—in this case, another two years] is what we talked about. No parole. No fines.

No counseling. No fees, etc. And I don't have to worry about my selfish uncles calling my parole officer and having me sent back to prison.

CHAPTER 10

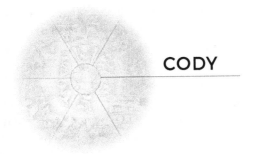

CODY

Name: Cody Griffin

Date of Birth: March 8, 1986

Education: GED

Family: One daughter

Prison Time: Sentenced in 2011 to life in prison without parole for capital murder. Previously served four years for other crimes.

Roy

I won't forget the day I met Cody. He was just being released from the Hole and was put into a cell right next to me. When I walked to the door to see what was going on, he looked up at me and he looked like he didn't have a friend in the world. He had a look of hopeless despair. I saw the loneliness in his face and body language—a look of total defeat. My heart was trying to tell his heart not to give up. I remember feeling in my heart it would be a miracle if the kid lasted to Christmas. I saw that he was giving up.

But there was no f–ing way I was going to let that kid give up. I threw him a cup of coffee and started to draw him out to get him to open up if possible in order to see where to start. That's when he had me feeling so beyond blessed and fortunate to have the family I have. There was death and sadness everywhere in his life. Cody's older sister committed suicide and his older brother died not long after. His dad was killed and his Mom died just as he went into the Hole. He had been watching her slowly kill herself with cigarettes and emphysema while suffering all the time. The family he did have didn't care. His older [half-] brother ain't said ten words to him since the murder happened. His younger sister has run off to San Antonio and probably won't ever say hello to him again. And, he realized he had only had two or three real friends in his life and one of them died and he didn't know how to find the other. So, basically, I was almost right about him, but was determined to help him beat the despair and lessen his suffering.

I could see he was thinking life was over. I could hear the suffering in his voice. It was a "no life" voice. Slowly, moment by moment, hour by hour, day by day, I shared the awesomeness and coolness, the WOW, of the Buddha's teachings and how much of an amazing change it had made in my heart and mind. I told him how, after only a couple of years meditating and studying and working the Dharma in every moment, I became blessed because I was suddenly aware that I was now experiencing a peace of mind, a freedom in the mind, that I had never come close to on the streets where I had had plenty of money to buy whatever I wanted. The koolness of Buddha's teachings had worked a miracle in my own life. That's when I had quit shooting dope. I told Cody how easy it was to let go of dope too. The more I shared the Dharma the more it began to take hold.

I'm glad we got to him before it was, well, not "too late," but before he could be overcome with negativity. Some of these guys, especially the young ones, are so full of hate, so full of self. They thrive on chaos and rebelliousness. They are full of "I can raise more hell than you" mentality and that combined with drugs gets you chaos for real—negative karma without question.

Moment by moment Cody has been working on strengthening his practice and I'm real proud of how he has handled his recent SNAFU that got him put in the Hole. He took advantage of his 30 days in the Hole and used it as a retreat and helped whoever, however, whenever he could. There's not a doubt in my heart or mind that if it weren't for the Dharma he would be dead or close to it. Out of all the dudes I've shared Buddha's teachings with, Cody is the most enthused as he didn't just enjoy the novelty of it. He digs the life Buddha put back in his heart. Cody will be carrying the torch for others to see so he won't be wasting that life sentence.

Cody

I was born in Paris, Arkansas, on March 8, 1986 at 4:30 p.m. My mother's name was Glenda Griffin and my dad's name was Shane Griffin. My birth name is Cody Shane Griffin. I had two sisters and two brothers. My dad died in a car wreck when I was 16. My older sister was in a bad marriage and she killed herself when I was 17. My older brother had a heart attack and passed away when I was 18.

We lived in a small, two-bedroom house and I was a wild kid. I remember my mom taking us to the store and her sitting in the car with me. When my sister went into the store I would climb out the window and run into the store after her. Growing up I would watch my brothers and sisters steal candy and stuff. Being young, I didn't know better so I started doing what I was seeing them do. I wish I had never gone on because I messed up my life.

My dad and mom left each other and I moved with my mom to a really small town called Branch, Arkansas. My mom never really cared what my sisters and brothers did. I was 7 years old and would run around to a friend's house and play and stay gone all day. When I was home I saw too many bad things for a 7 year old. Older friends of my mom's drank, smoked weed, had sex, and I was not getting food. But at school it was bad too and when we had Christmas it would be a church bringing bags and presents because my mom didn't have money for them.

One day when I was 7, I was outside playing and I had a cigarette lighter and was playing with fire. There was a church close to our house and it had a big trash can. I got to playing with it and it caught on fire and there were wooden steps with leaves on the church. When the trash blew over the leaves, they caught on fire and the side of the church caught fire. I ran across the street and was scared and was hiding. A woman saw me and told the firemen and they got me and the police called DHS, and they took me away from my mom for not taking care of me.

I went with a couple named Tina and Wendell. They were a nice young family who lived in Cecil, Arkansas, and were Baptists. They took really good care of me and got me nice new clothes. They didn't have any kids because they couldn't have any. They got me into school and I was doing much better. They didn't let me run around or walk around where I wanted; they were real strict. Wendell signed me up for baseball and taught me how to play. I think I was 9 years old by then. He was a cool father figure. For one of my birthdays he got me a BB gun and started teaching me to hunt. He taught me to help out around the house too, and I would cut the grass and keep the yard clean. He also bought me a 4-10 shotgun for deer hunting and showed me how to hunt. But when we went hunting, I would get tired of sitting and just shoot the gun and act like I shot at a deer just to get home.

Wendell was a welder in Fort Smith, Arkansas, at a shop that made the pitchforks for hay tractors. He had an accident and a metal beam fell and killed him. I remember the day it happened because his wife didn't pick me up at school, her sister did. She took me to her house and told me that I was going to get to go home and visit my mom for a while and that Wendell had been hurt and was in a better place. I didn't know at the time he had passed away. Later, when Tina told me about Wendell, it hurt me because he taught me so much. They had planned to adopt me but it was hard on Tina losing Wendell so I went back to my mom, who had moved to Horatio, Arkansas.

My dad had got back with my mom and things were a lot better for us. Plus, I had learned a lot from Tina and Wendell. It was like my dad was a new man. He worked and took care of us like he was supposed to, and for my 12th birthday I got a horse and was into cowboy stuff and wanted to learn calf roping, so my dad worked with me every day and I got into the school rodeo. I won second place in my first rodeo and first place in team roping. When I left school each day, I went straight to my horse, saddled him up, and stayed on him until my mom started calling me Polo and soon after that I named my horse Marco.

By the time I was 14 years old, my dad got to drinking more and was not spending that much time with me. He and my mom were fighting a lot more and my brothers and sisters were moving out and were done with school. Then, when I was 16 going on 17 years old my dad had a bad car wreck going to work and was killed. I found out when I got home from school and saw the cops at my house. It crushed me badly and my life started going down-hill from there.

I sold my horse and was getting into smoking pot and drinking every day with a whole new group of friends. I gave up rodeo and started staying out all night and began dating. I smoked weed with this girl; her dad sold weed and I began hanging out with homeboys who liked to party every day. When we didn't have money, one of the dudes would break into houses and steal stuff and sell it to buy beer, pot, pills, or whatever the girls liked.

On Thanksgiving Day I arrived at my mom's house to find her crying and I found out that my older sister Tonya was dead from taking a bunch of pills. I ran to her house where she had a brother who did meth. That day I smoked it for the first time and loved it because it gave me so much energy. I got my other three buddies to try it and we would smoke it and be up for five to ten days without sleep or food.

Then one of the dudes who stole stuff broke into the house next to my mom's and stole guns and a lot of stuff and put it all behind my house but didn't tell me where he got it. So I helped him bring the stuff through my window and a few hours later the police arrived and asked to talk to me. My mother let them come in to look around and when they got to my room and saw the dude, he jumped out the window and ran. They took me to jail and charged me with residential burglary and theft based upon receiving the stolen goods and I went to prison for the first time for a couple of years.

When I got out I lived with and took care of my mom and got a job, but I still had my problems with drugs. I was fine at work, but when I got home and thought about my family passing away, I would smoke a little weed or if there was a lot of stuff I needed to do, I would do some meth to get my mind off of what I had to do but found out it would all come back later.

I have to admit it was hard getting on my feet. For a time I lived with my sister and her old man because he had an auto shop and I could do some work there and help out with the bills. The auto shop was next door to a nice old house and my plan was to fly good and get my own house. But before I knew it I started f–ing up. I went out with this girl who had her own house and wanted me to move in with her. She wanted me to be around 24/7, and I didn't like that. It was nice to have what I wanted but she did not make me happy. One day when she was gone I packed up all my stuff in my truck and went to my homeboy's house. He lived in Gillam, Arkansas.

I got a job at Tyson's chicken plant and the owner gave me money to rent an apartment until I got my paycheck. The apartment building was run down and there were drugs flowing there. Before long my stuff was stolen out of my apartment while I was at work. My buddy said I could stay with him and his girl if I shared rent. We worked right next to each other at Tyson's and we got high all the time on weed.

My buddy's girl liked to do meth and I started liking it again and was going to work high and staying up for 6 days at a time. After I lost weight and was down to 115 pounds I stopped doing meth and worked and saved up and had a Chevy truck with a three-inch lift on it and some mud-slinger tires. It was a beast. One day I was getting ice [meth] and a 30-pack of Bud Light when Autumn pulled up in a truck next to me and told me she liked my truck. It was love at first sight and I ended up moving in with her and her aunt and uncle and grandma.

Then I got Autumn and I a place and had it for a year or two when something happened at work. I cut my index finger almost all the way off and they drug tested me and found out I had been smoking weed so I lost my job and Autumn and I moved back in with her relatives. At the time my mom was sick and not doing well and it hurt me seeing her sick like that so I started smoking weed more and drinking more and I had fights with Autumn. Finally I got a job at a Pizza Hut where there was a pretty supervisor and after I started as a dishwasher she was always back there flirting with me.

One day I was too drunk to listen to Autumn telling me I shouldn't go mudding in my truck when I was drunk. I didn't listen. I went to a big mud hole and ended up stuck in it. I blew my motor up trying to get out and that left me without a truck to get to work. I had to bum rides to work and the girl who hired me told me she'd give me a ride. Autumn didn't like it because this girl was smoking hot. I flirted with her, thinking that would help me get a shift supervisor job. Once I got drunk with her and she got arrested so I bailed her out. After that, Autumn left me and went to live with her mother. I stayed with my sister for a few weeks until Autumn talked to me again. Then she was pregnant. I was happy as hell and one day at the doctor's office got to hear baby Blossom's heart beat.

I got work out of town with my brother and when I got back, I heard that Autumn was with someone else, her X. When I saw her, she said I needed a full-time job before she would talk with me again. I got back to doing dope—meth—and had been up for 20 days without sleep or food and felt like no one loved me. It was late one night when my sister caught me smoking meth in her house and told me to get out. I had no money and made up my mind to rob a store where they had money in a safe. I was high. I didn't have a mask on and was not in my right mind. The young woman opened the store and I went in behind her with a knife and grabbed her and told her to open the safe. It had a lot of money in it and I put it in a bag and told her she was going to drive me to the other side of town. When we got in the car I had the knife in my hand and I reached over to grab her seat belt to put it on her and yanked it down and she jumped and the knife cut the main vein in her neck. She passed away and I was scared. I put her in the trunk when I got to the country and hid. A helicopter was out looking for me. They had me on camera. I didn't want to live when I saw the cop coming and wanted him to shoot me, tried to get him to shoot me, but he wouldn't. I told them what happened and went to jail where I tried to kill myself with a sheet tied to the bars of my cell. But I just passed out and woke up in the hospital and here I am now. That's my life, Bro'.

I was sent to prison October 9th for murder and was sentenced to life without parole. I was 25 years old and I'm 26 years old now. My mom was my best friend. She wrote me every week when I came to prison and sent me $100.00 every month. Before I came to prison my mom's cancer was getting bad and she lived with my aunt who was helping take care of her. I was in my cell when the officer came to take me to the Chaplin's office and he told me to call my aunt. She told me my mom got bad and went to the hospital and passed away. I blamed it a lot on myself because of putting stress on my mom for what I did that got me in prison.

The fact is that I'm in prison for the rest of my life. I have a brother on the run from the law. My sister has two kids and one of them is in a wheelchair. She has so much going on in her life that she can't worry about me and I have a little girl named Blossom. At the time I was locked up, my girlfriend Autumn was only four months pregnant. Autumn couldn't come to see me because she is a felon. I didn't have anyone to bring Blossom to see me.

Doug

I read the last half of your life story before prison—it is a heartbreaker for sure. So much suffering.

In your new life, I think of what I sent Roy: Preach what you practice. Each moment you and I practice. The practice is what is essential. Sharing with others about the Buddha can be very helpful, but others should see the practice as well as hear the words. If you are going to practice kindness and letting go, you must be aware of what you are practicing each moment. I make mistakes, so I assume you will too. I try not to get down on myself.

As I said before, I believe you can help the other youngsters. Always interested in hearing about your preaching what you practice.

Cody

After a few weeks [at Tucker] no one was writing to me. I felt like I had nobody anymore to write me or send me a little money every now and then. It hurt me bad and still hurts me now. I was in my cell about two weeks after hearing about my mother [dying of emphysema] and wanted to watch NASCAR because I'm a big fan, but they put on basketball. I let my anger get the best of me and I set my cell on fire and went to the Hole for 30 days and that is when I got out and met the coolest dude ever—his name is Roy Tester and he is in the cell next to me and he let me check out a book on Buddhism called *Effortless Meditation* and it's cool as f–. Roy is a good teacher for me. He's always telling me to "Let it go" because I'm 26 years old and tend to let things get at me.

· · · · · · · ·

After reading about supports for mindfulness, Roy had to break it down for me. I came up with me cleaning my cell. Instead of rushing through it and just wiping down the sink and toilet and sweeping the floor with the broom and mop that has been in 53 cells, I now take a rag and soap and I sweep with a rag and then I get down on my hands and knees and wipe the walls. I also scrub the floor and get the corners really good. I also take time in wiping my bed down and putting clean sheets on it and by doing this and taking my time I get to take in the good clean floor and toilet and the smell of clean sheets on my bed. When you have a good clean cell it makes you feel better and cleaner inside.

· · · · · · · ·

You blew me away when you told me on the phone that my letters help you too. Well that makes me feel good. It makes me feel like I actually am somebody, because being 26 years old and having lost my mom and dad means I have nobody to write me at all. And, I'm doing a Life Without so it's really hard to wake up every day to face another day when there will be no word from family or loved ones. I think about my baby girl and hope she and Autumn are safe and making it.

Saturday my baby girl, Blossom, turned five months old, so she was on my mind a lot and it got me in a sad frame of mind and it was not making anything better thinking about how I f–ed up and left her like I did. So I took a low, deep, slow breath and kissed her picture and said that daddy will do good to others so I can have good karma back for the both of us. So the kindness I show, I push myself to show times two for me and Blossom.

. . . .

I tend to ask myself all the time: what do I have to be joyful about? I've begun to realize my answer is: Everything! Everything is joy to me. I'm alive, I'm facing my difficulties and I'm actually living my life the best I can and not hiding from my pain. I realize too that I'm just happy to be alive. I'm happy to be here where I can talk, laugh, and smile. It's not delusion or hiding or shutting down in denial; it's being present and taking things one moment at a time. If I sit around and feel sorry for myself and think about my mom and dad and every bitty thing that has passed away and what I don't have, then it's hard to find joy.

. . . .

Well, they moved Roy into the cell right next to me again. That's crazy because it's hard to get put next to the same person in here. He is in bad shape. I'm trying to help him out and take care of him as best I can and keep him in a good mind. They don't want to help him out at all.

Thank you for the money. I have plenty of stamps now and I bought myself and a few people ice cream and helped them out. My buddy, he doesn't have any family so I got him a t-shirt and it was nice to see the smiles on their faces. Thanks for your teaching in kindness. I can enjoy spreading the kindness and showing the good heart that I truly have.

I was talking to Roy and I want to get out and go to population because I'm tired of just sitting in this cell. I've been locked up one year now and I really want to work on maintenance crew, but Roy is my Buddy and I want to be there to holler for help if he needs it. There is other stuff I help him do since his hands are bad, though it would be really good for Roy to get out and go to population. He just sits back here in the cell all day. Roy thinks I would be better off going to population and getting a job and spreading the Dharma by sharing letting go and showing kindness is "kool" by helping folks write letters or listening to someone who needs to talk. He says he's still too physically impaired to be out there around a bunch of people.

Roy

Cody went to disciplinary court just an hour or so ago and got totally f–ed over, just like I did.

Cody has been having some heavy f–ing seizures the last couple of weeks that are bad enough he gave himself a concussion, busted his lip open, blackened his eyes, and busted open a couple of places above his eye and on his head. If I didn't know differently, there is no way you could convince me the guards didn't beat him down.

The seizure was so bad the following night that they had to transport him to UAMS [University of Arkansas for Medical Sciences] in Little Rock to the Emergency Room. They did a blood test that showed the only thing in him was his prescribed medicines. No drugs, nothing. The doctor, a bona fide doctor, wrote out a statement saying there was no way Cody could be expected to piss. No way. And what happens? They gave him 30 days Hole time and 60 days restriction [because he was incapable of producing urine for a urine test]. Tell me that ain't hateful.

Cody

I went to the doctor and he told me I got to see a neurologist because when the scan came back it showed I have a spot in my brain and I think it's a tumor but I don't know. I have to be honest. I was scared at first and wanted to call you about it, but then I did meditation and let it go. They've got me on seizure meds now and when you get this I will only have five days left in the Hole.

. . . .

It's like when life gets to getting better for me, something happens and it pulls me through the mud again. I started a new medicine and was given two shots today, but afterwards it makes me feel weak and I don't want to do anything but lay here and cry. I keep telling myself to pick my head up and "Let it go," but it is so f–ing hard. It's like this tumor is me getting punished for the crime I did.

. . . .

I just wanted to let you know that the teachings of Buddhism have really opened my eyes. For example, when I talk with the other guys here, even the guards, I listen and let them just talk and I can see their joy and frustration and anger. I really dig being mindful. This last month has just brought me so much WOW. You know, it's like when I got the Christmas package that I thank you so much for. When I got the package, I put everything on my bed and took everything in my mind, from the point I filled out the form to sending it to you and you calling it in and the people that packed it together and its trip here. Then I thought about all the smiles and how each item that I send to someone would bring joy. All I asked in a letter when I sent the gifts was to be kind to someone in some way and to keep the kindness going.

Facing Reality

This life without parole—BAM—hits you like an 18-wheeler smack in prison ... Every day we are set to go through the day by waking up at 2:00 a.m., eating breakfast, and then going back to sleep until 9:30 a.m., eating lunch and then back down. Almost everybody stays up all night and sleeps all day. Well this is how I have started my day: I sleep all night and eat chow at 2 a.m., and then I meditate for at least 15 minutes. During the 15 minutes I go through a lot of body scanning and start over and over and get zoned out and I'm really feeling calm. I realize I should do it more. A lot of my problem is laziness. I have been on a good diet and I weigh 193 lbs. I was 240 lbs. and it was my goal to lose, and I did it. After I meditate I go back to sleep, then when I get up again I go through the little work out plan I started and so 20 sets of 10 pushups, then 10 sets of lunges and 20 sets of crunches. When I finish around 12:00 p.m., I walk around my cell and do a lot of walking meditation by letting a lot of thoughts go. I do this by focusing upon my steps, counting them and breathing slow. Then I eat at 2:30 p.m., chill and take a shower. I have a toilet in my cell that has a shower and it's really helpful. Then I put my mat on the concrete slab to sleep.

PART III
THE STRUGGLE

CHAPTER 11

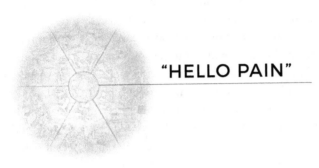

"HELLO PAIN"

Roy

One day I was fit as a fiddle, in great shape and working in the bakery at night. I paused in my job to help a friend, the meat cook. He had two carts of chicken boxes full of frozen food needing to be unloaded. I jumped to it, grabbing boxes weighing approximately 60 lbs. and slinging them over by the big steam pots. Halfway through, I slung one wrong, and felt a sharp stabbing pain in my lower back. Then after a few seconds, I said, "Nuttin' 2it" and finished unloading. By midnight I was hurting so bad I had to go back to the block. I've been in pain ever since and had two surgeries. Can I find joy in these difficult times? You betcha. Ain't easy, but good things in life don't come easy.

. . . .

The orthopedic surgeon who operated on me and did my spinal fusion told my doctor here he wouldn't operate on me again because it would only make me worse and possibly even paralyze me because my body is creating so much scar tissue. That's the kind of news one has to come to terms with and let go of.

Now I've had another challenge thrown at me. The specialist on my last visit said my skeleton is collapsing, and he means it literally. I'll probably be in a wheelchair within three years. I will have more pinching of my nerves, like the one in my neck that is tweaking down my left arm, making tactile sensations difficult. There's not much pain, just numbness, deep numbness.

. . . .

I've got some unkool developments with my old breaking down vehicle. I'm losing feeling in my left hand to the point where I can't use it, Bro. I can't open a pack of crackers or squeeze toothpaste out. Some hours it can be so intense I can't pick up a vitamin or button my pants. That's followed by 30 minutes of fairly good use, then comes a whole 24 hours of just total numb, excruciating pain in my hand. The knot on my spine between my shoulder blades has gotten bigger and super sensitive to touch. The nurse said it sounds like not only a pinched nerve, but also possibly an infection. ...

My liver is causing problems [as a result of Hepatitis C]. My feet and legs are swollen up more than they've ever been. The skin on my feet and ankles is so tight it feels like it's going to split open, and up to my knees it is like I have one long thigh from my crotch down to my ankles.

Why is this happening, all this physical unkoolness, culminating in hell on earth? If it weren't for my practice, I don't think I could deal with this.

....

Sorry this is so hard to read. I have to learn to use my left hand to write with, and as you can see it's kind of raw. It was frustrating not being able to talk with you on the phone. I needed to hear you tell me that everything would be okay. Someone back here in the Hole, which is where I am, obviously took out his anger on the phone so no one else could use it. I'm f–ing scared I'll never get to use my right hand normally again. I found out that the pain clinic turned me down and on top of that, not being able to use my right hand is a heavy blow.

....

I sleep most of the time sitting up, drooped over my table or up on my bed, leaning back against the wall because lying down f–ing sucks. Sometimes it takes a while for me to recognize that pain has taken control of my mind, my every thought.

I'm thinking a billion thoughts, useless and negative. I'm not doing mantras, reciting prayers, or generating merit for anyone, not checking in on any of my amigos in here to see if they need some cheering up because they still haven't heard from their families. I'm only focused on me, my pain, my suffering.

John

As for Roy, I can tell you his pain is deep. I am not in his barracks, but the other morning they took two of us over to their shower stalls to speed the showers up. I saw Roy with his head on the table, face first, legs leaning sideways, one arm dangling off the table. I called to him a few times. Our showers are only ten minutes, though. He finally woke up, but we had only about three minutes before they came for me. He had a nice new scar on his head where he had passed out against the bars. His voice was groggy and slurred. I told him that you wrote me concerned about him. He said he had written. He thought?? I know he's lost a lot of weight. I'd say he weighs 90 lbs. He won't answer my kites either.

Now I cry when I get a glimpse of him or ask the guards about him. Inside the man is still a man, but outside he is failing. And I know, just as you do, what it's like being a man losing your physical abilities and how it makes you feel less than a man.

He's still my friend though, no matter what. I love him like a brother I never had.

Roy

As each day passes I gain a deeper respect for my uncle who was a paraplegic who I used to help do everything from flushing out his kidneys with a big eye [dropper] looking thing, like a turkey baster that I filled up with some purple stuff. He would squirt it into his catheter, then release the pressure, which would fill up with the ugly looking stuff. It would take a full gallon to flush his kidneys.

I don't have it near as challenging as my uncle because his hands were claws. He couldn't write without a special made brace on, and even then his writing was real shaky but he overcame the battles. Forgive me for talking about a private subject, but you need to fully understand the situation with my hands. To write, I'm not able to really squeeze my pen. But when I have to go to the toilet and have to wipe, I've been trying to put it off but it gets to hurting so bad I have no choice. And it couldn't be an easy movement with no mess. No, it would be just like Uncle Harbo. I had an advantage over him because I got a lot of control over fingers compared to him and I'm whining. I thought things were going to be easy, but when I got to the toilet I slipped first and got shit all over my hand. I had already spilled a cup of coffee because of a muscle spasm and had pissed in the bed because I had lain flat and had been trying to get up when something happened and I pissed all over myself. I finally got up and just sat on the f–ing toilet and cried.

I was crying because I had shit all over my hand but I was also remembering the time as a nine-year-old kid when I was helping my uncle wipe his ass, and he always had a messy movement, but he had gotten over the embarrassment. I didn't look at it as f–ed up either. The first time he hollered for me to help him, he asked and said I didn't have to and that pissed me off. I remember it too. I told him I'm more f–ing grown up than he thought and we got it done.

· · · · · · · ·

I've never felt such cold, even when I froze my hands riding a train in December through Wisconsin and Minnesota. My hands froze then because I did a shot of heroin and didn't have on gloves so I could do the shot. When I came to, my arm up to my elbow was hell, but the pain I suffered then isn't as cruel as this nerve damage shit. Writing to you hurts like hell but I'm just doing it in defiance. You know, like "F– you Pain!!" Come on with it! Hurt me! Come on!

I'm seriously off my center. It has had my mind f–ed up because my anger came back with a vengeance when my pain starting spiking the meter. I've been snappin' at people and actually having a murderous heart. I was so furious a couple of times when a nurse wouldn't give me a shot of Toradol for pain that I was describing all the ways I would love to kill her family members—kids and all—none would be spared, no one, and that nurse would be alive on the planet with no family, alone. I would cripple them so bad they'd be like ol' Superman, Christopher Reeves.

· · · · · · · ·

It kills me to say this to you, but I have bought some meds to put with my own stuff to try to get some relief for just a couple of hours. I'm not looking for whole days, but just a couple of hours. I am ashamed to tell you this after I went so many years without doing that kind of shit. I went from being a good, strong example for Buddha to being a piece of shit. I'm sorry for letting you all down and being such a disappointment.

· · · · · · · ·

I know it's just pain and have broken it down bit by bit to know that resisting and fighting pain will increase the intensity in a major way every f–in' time, so, the key is to just see it for what it is and let it be, let it go, let go of attachment to the pain. Every time, though, when the pain would spike way worse than the present moment, Letting Go was history.

When it gets to where I'm just crying from pain, all I can do then is visualize Chenrezig [the goddess of compassion] slowly becoming brighter and brighter, but with a soft brightness, not a harsh glare. As I continuously chant the compassion mantra I visualize Chenrezig's light slowly transforming my bulky physical form with all its pain until we're both just one pure, soft, super bright light shining Loving-kindness and compassion to the whole world, comforting those who are suffering.

. . . .

Now, to put a little bit more difficulty into the mix, do this with your back screaming mad because you just did some serious damage with your slip and fall [on the wet floor] and you ain't feeling but about 30 percent due to a recent sick spell from your old friend hepatitis and it's not until late evening on Saturday before you've got the energy to write. My feet are starting to get out of control again but, no worries, because I will get it under control again as always. Warrior spirit? Yes indeed my friend.

. . . .

I've been working on a poem about my pain. I'm sure as hell not a poet so bear with me please:

> Pain
> Ha! Hello Pain.
> Yeah I know you're there;
> So what?!
> You don't scare me!
> You don't rule me!
> You empower me!
> You strengthen my resolve!
> You help me and
> Pain, yeah,
> You teach me.
> So thank you.

Well, that's it Bro. First poem for me. After I read a couple you sent a couple of months back it was as if well, like I was letting pain do all the talking, so now I'm talking back, but in a courteous manner.

When my pain starts dominating my existence, when it becomes the only thing in my thoughts and when I finally really have to "buckle up," I look to all my Buddhas and bow to each one and ask for strength to overcome the pain so I can learn more of his teaching which will help me help others. I make Self step aside. I become focused on others. If I'm focused on pain then it's pretty much for sure I won't have a smile on my face. Sometimes a smile might be all it takes to help someone's day become bearable. I can't let pain interfere with helping others! If I'm focused upon pain, then my readiness with a kind word is hindered! Thoughts like these, Bro, help me deal with my pain. I'm a warrior, my friend. Pain helps keep me tough.

· · · · · · · ·

Meditation is like putting a battery on a charger. I come out of a "sitting" and can read and study or do other stuff for a bit without being distracted by pain.

· · · · · · · ·

I simply refuse to let this pain I deal with 24/7 make me into a bad, uncaring, unloving, and uncool person. I will not become a slave to hatefulness. This pain has helped me in every way as it is a constant reminder—a post-it note—telling me to love, not hate, to be kind and compassionate, not hateful. I think of [the great Soto Zen teacher] Shunryu Suzuki's "correction stick"— that little loving tap is intended to give you confidence to overcome whatever obstacle is confronting you. My pain is also my comfort, if that makes sense at all. The guards and nurses who are consumed with hatefulness, bitterness, and anger when I'm confronted with them are that "little tap" from Suzuki's stick. To react to their hatefulness with hatefulness would be to let them win; it would be like letting them control my mind, letting them become my master. They can control me physically, but mentally and spiritually I'll not let them control me. Hopefully when they see me react to their hatefulness with kindness and compassionate understanding and with Koolness, Buddha's Koolness, it will plant some tiny seed within their hearts.

· · · · · · · ·

There were four guards who went out of their way to come to the infirmary to check on me. They stayed late just to talk with me. Yeah, there is compassion in this compound of anger and hate.

· · · · · · · ·

When Administration put me in lock up, or what is known as administrative segregation, because of my physical condition, it really didn't bother me because it doesn't matter where I'm housed doing a life without parole sentence; it's all prison. I'm always going to be fairly close to other inmates, which means I'm always going to be able to show kindness in one form or another. Spreading kindness and joy is part of my Dharma Pain Management.

CHAPTER 12

FACING THE DARKNESS

Roy called and told me about his health issues, which were severe enough to get him moved from the Hole to the infirmary. Pinched nerves were causing numbness in both hands and sharp pain in his neck when he looked up. He could not straighten his fingers. Without his hands he could not write or hold a book to read it. He was frantic about losing the use of his hands. Prison doctors said they'd keep an eye on the problem, and refused to authorize an MRI or CT scan.

While in the infirmary, Roy was also treated for swelling in his right leg, which was three times its normal size and causing his skin to split. He was treated with antibiotics and then treated with a second round when the swelling returned. He later told me that on his first day in the infirmary, he slept from 6 a.m. to 8 p.m. and woke up dreaming of [the famous Zen teacher and peace activist] Thich Nhat Hanh.

Although he feared it could result in retaliation from the medical staff at Tucker, Roy's pain and worsening disability was so great that he asked me to go over their heads and contact the Arkansas Department of Corrections Medical Services Office. Linda and I began calling the office of the medical medical director for the prison system. After calling several times, we heard back from her executive assistant saying the director would look into Roy's case. A week later, we heard from Roy that the Tucker medical department had ordered new pain medication and a CT scan for him. He was ecstatic.

Linda and I assumed that our efforts were to thank for the change, but the next day I received a letter from Roy that gave the rest of the story. It turns *out, a nurse who thought highly of Roy had intervened, writing a request that he be seen for a second opinion and making sure her request stayed at the top of the doctor's stack of paperwork. In the end, we realized that more than our intervention, Roy's loving-kindness and respect toward his fellow inmates and the prison staff had made the real difference.*

Roy

Well, I've got more than kneecap pain Bro. When I went for my x-rays Friday and was trying to get off the x-ray table I dislocated my knee even worse than the half dozen times before. Miss Carswell, my doctor, was super pissed off at the nurse for not paying attention to what she was doing, which was supposed to be helping me off the x-ray table. She was more focused on talking on a portable phone than on holding the stool stable so I could step down on it then step down to the floor. The Doc was just walking by the x-ray room and she saw what was going to happen a split second before it did, but knew there was nothing she could do to stop it. She apologized a dozen times even though it wasn't her fault. She did put a letter of reprimand in the nurse's jacket because she had been warned about using the phone for personal calls and doing it this time caused someone to get hurt even worse than they were to begin with.

· · · · · · · ·

Yesterday at the N.L.R [North Little Rock] hospital, where the CT scan took place, I had to lay down on a hard surface for the CT. It had me in tears in just a couple of minutes but I had to be perfectly still so as not to f– the scan up. It took barely six minutes totally, but I had to have three people help me up and then they started getting concerned. One person who has known me for years said, "Shit, Tester, I never realized you were this f–ed up." Then we got in the van and went over big speed bumps; they were easy to see, but the driver was talking on a cell phone and not paying attention or being mindful at all. She hit the first bump so hard my head hit the roof of the van and it felt like I was poked with a cattle prod in my neck that shot down both my arms to my fingers. I started yelling and cussing her and telling her to get off the phone. It was totally out of my character as it had no Loving-kindness, no dharma, just anger at this Sgt.'s stupidity, which was causing so much pain. Bro, she didn't even hear me because she had ear buds from her phone crammed deep into her ears. The other Sgt. apologized for her hitting the speed bump, but before he could finish, she hit another one. Harder than the first time. Bro, I thought I was going to piss my pants or shit my pants or both because the pain was so bad in my neck. I couldn't even cuss at her or talk. The other Sgt. actually snatched the ear bud from her ear and told her she better get her head back at work and to put her phone down or he would write her up. That's when she realized what she'd done. She heard and saw me crying, but instead of compassion, she simply said, "Shit, you should have been ready for my bad driving over those speed bumps." I remained silent for the rest of the 45-minute trip back to the prison.

· · · · · · · ·

I've just went through four days of having no pain meds because of the deliberate indifference of a very hateful nurse who, when I complained by way of a grievance, came all the way to my blocks to tell me, "Look you piece of shit, I don't give a damn if you ever get any pain medicine. I know why you're in prison and you'll never suffer enough to make up for what you did you sick f–. So f– you and your grievances and just try to prove I've said what I did." Now, ain't that some shit? When I calmly said, "I feel so sorry for you Ma'am," she got even more pissed off than she was and started yelling at me saying stuff like, "I don't give a f– about you feeling sorry for me because I damn sure as hell don't feel anything but hate for you, you piece of shit, and I guarantee you're going to go without your precious pain meds more than you do manage to get them."

Bro', she Lost it, and f–ed up when she did because the only Lieutenant here who still treats us with the same respect he does for free world folks and will stand up for you all the way if he believes you're in the right heard what she was yelling. When she turned around to walk off he was standing right behind her! He told her she might as well go to the infirmary, get her little lunch bucket and whatever else she brought and get the f– down the highway because he heard everything she said. That was a wonderful moment Bro. She had deliberately let my pain meds run out. That nurse went straight back to the infirmary for her stuff, told her boss she just didn't feel safe working here, and left. The Lt. went down there a few minutes after she took off and told her boss what really happened and then told him he needed to get his shit together because we were still human beings and regardless of our crime, we deserved the same level of professionalism that he expected in the free world. The inmate porter told me everything that the Lt. said.

· · · · · · · ·

Yesterday I was supposed to be going back to see a doctor, a specialist who came here, but a certain guard who is a racist, hateful female came to take me but didn't have the wheelchair. She knows I have to use it to travel any distance more than a few feet, so she acted like she didn't know and said, "Oh, I'll get to you later." She is also mad at me for something that's her own doing. She got caught in a lie to a superior officer because she doesn't like white people. I got tired of begging her for a property box. She wouldn't even acknowledge me, my "request," because I'm white. She doesn't hesitate to help her own race. I got tired of it. I asked a white Lieutenant who I've known for many years for help. She lied in his face, saying she didn't have any boxes and even lied to an Assistant Warden too. When he told me she said she didn't have any, I told him where she kept some new ones for her homies. When he busted her out for lying, she in turn got real petty and vindictive and kept me from being able to see the specialist by putting me off until the specialist left. I could get her in big trouble for this but have managed to get rescheduled for the specialist without getting her in further trouble and possible termination. I had to meditate and really focus on Buddha's teachings before my anger faded. Once I decided to have compassion for her, I felt like a weight had been lifted off my heart. Some of the fellas who knew about it were trying to get me to burn her by filing charges but when I said no and told them how I was handling it they said, "Man, she still gonna hate you, try to f– you over," and I said, "Maybe, but what matters is my actions for my karma. What matters is where my heart's at." They told me I was stronger than they were. Buddha didn't say following his teachings was going to be easy and I do feel stronger because of the way I handled it.

· · · · · · · · ·

I was told yesterday I will no longer get my pain meds three times daily. From now on it's going to be two times a day. The head doctor has never seen me nor examined me and has decided I no longer need the meds three times a day. I was without methadone from Friday 5 p.m. to Monday 6:15 p.m. [the doctor] was here early a.m. and had she cared just a little bit I could have had a dose by 10 a.m. and she was aware of my situation. By 8:30 a.m. a guard I trust went to the infirmary and told [the director] and the nurse, but [the doctor who gave the order] told him, "He'll be okay." A nurse who has helped me so much did her call and gave me my meds and then tried to apologize for the cruelness of [the doctor] and the maggot above her. She said she couldn't deal with such ugly hearted people any more. She said her heart hurt too much at the end of the day. She apologized for not being able to help me more and hoped that I would be able to forgive her for quitting. When I told her there was nothing to forgive her for, that I had love and respect for her that I couldn't put into words, she started crying. When she didn't come back for the last pill call at 3 p.m. the nurse that came with the meds said Miss K came back from pill call and said she couldn't be part of the f–ing ugliness anymore.

When [the doctor] came out of her office and asked Miss K what her problem was, Nurse Forrest said Miss K went off on her. Well, she exploded and called [the doctor] a cold-hearted bitch who had betrayed her oath and was a true hypocrite who someday would pay dearly for selling her honor.

John

Well, [the doctor] who was seeing Roy, has got herself, along with the Head Supervisor, D.O.N., the A.P.N. and half the staff, in a lawsuit. They are being forced to resign and are in for one heck of a lawsuit that will take their license. Short story is that they got in trouble and came in one night and deleted an inmate's files out of all the computers. What they didn't know is the inmate had got copies before they deleted [the originals]. Plus, as you know, when the Feds step in they are going to step in and confiscate the computers to check the hard drives, so as you see, Roy was telling the truth about the infirmary. There are six people right now filing lawsuits. [The staff will] lose their licenses and get brought up on criminal charges, federal charges and not only fined, but possibly prison time.

Roy

Yesterday, Sat. night, about 5 minutes to 9 p.m. I got out of bed feeling bad, hurting and truly miserable in pain, got to the toilet but just as I started pissin', I blacked out and fell right straight down on my tail bone. Hit so hard [when] I snapped back to consciousness I was pissing on myself and the breath knocked out of me from the severity of the impact to my tail-bone. I could do nothin' but cry because any kind of bodily movement took my sight, yet my eyes were bug-eyed wild. Then it took concentration on my breathing to totally "Locked In" on slowing my breathing to a smooth rhythm, a smooth natural flow in and out. Once I got some of the shock to my spine under control I slowly retrieved my hard plastic plates, front and back (hard shell) back brace which I haven't worn in years. Wore it constantly for three days because I couldn't bear to move without that sucker strapped on tight. Had to Let go of the anger at myself for not being able to not piss on myself. Couldn't f–in' breathe and couldn't stop pissin' on myself. If it weren't for my practice I'd break weak and commit bye-bye.

· · · · · · · ·

There's a night shift nurse here who knows me pretty well and after I told him about the last couple of weeks being more painful than it ever has, my foot mostly, but in my back also, he told me I need to put as much energy as I possibly could into my practice because my pain is going to slowly get worse. I told him I already f–in' knew that. He said Yeah, but think about it. They're not going to increase your meds so you'd better have a back-up plan, meaning I had better learn to deal with my pain with Mindfulness. I need to harness the power of my mind and use it to keep my pain from driving me insane or worse.

Confession

Around the same time as Roy was threatening suicide, he wrote me a letter in which he confessed to two other murders, committed before the murders of his parents. I believe he may have wanted to get these killings off his chest before he died. I later told Roy that if I was going to include his confession in this book, I would have to report the crimes to authorities. He agreed, reiterating that he wanted them to be part of his story. I passed along the information to the attorneys general in the relevant states, and the crimes are now being investigated.

I was on the run on murder charges in Houston, Texas, doing smack every day, but also working six and seven days a week remodeling a 93-year-old house while living with a stripper. She got drunk one morning and showed me some photos. Her "ex" had beat the shit out of her more than once. He went to the joint in Texas for it. He nearly killed her. It turns out he f–in' gets out of prison on a technicality on appeal. She wasn't notified prior to his release.

At 6 p.m. I came home from working my ass off and had a tool belt on—18-ounce Eastwing framing hammer in the loop, screwdrivers and shit. Walking up on the porch I noticed the f–in' screen door barely hanging on one hinge and the main door kicked in, door jamb shattered. I heard her screaming and heard, then saw, this bully prick. Screaming "I'm fixin' to cut your f–in' head off" and I see a knife.

I felt there was only one choice for me to make. I slid that Eastwing with the straight claw out of my tool belt and took three long steps and sunk that mfkr in his head, killing him. I hit the correct part (luckily) of his brain because it froze the arm with the knife in it. He dropped to the floor but lived long enough to look in my face to see who had destroyed his hate-filled intentions. If I hadn't killed him, he would have killed her, cutting her head off for real. There would've been no reasoning with him. He had already beaten the shit out of her. He had been out of prison less than 24 hours with the full intention of cutting her head off. Bully prick was abusively ugly to everyone he encountered, but was a great con man/bullshitter.

I saved her life, plus no telling how many others, by killing him. I think I made the compassionate decision. What say you? Justified homicide or murder? Only three people are aware of this particular incident. Her, me, now you. I wrapped him in heavy concrete plastic, took him to where I was remodeling that house, and buried him beneath what became, the next day, a 15' x 22' patio. Later that week when I got paid, I told her I was going for a 6-pack and rolling papers and I left Houston. I know she never told anybody because I never heard any more about it. Yeh, I killed him, but he had an ugly heart and she was a beautiful-hearted chick.

· · · · · · · ·

New murder Bro, I actually stalked and tracked down a very violent, hateful man in Salt Lake, Utah. I was crashing on a back porch when all hell broke loose inside the house, which had the porch I was trespassing and crashing on. I heard physical contact, kids screaming, a woman begging the dude to just leave. Then I heard a punch and knew he had broken her jaw. I ran around to the front door in time to see this bully backhand a 10-year-old kid, which had her flying across the room. I grabbed a lamp off the end table and knocked him out.

It was a weird situation. I didn't know them and they didn't know me. I asked her if she had a car because if she didn't she'd have to go in an ambulance. Her jaw was broke, bad. Her little girl had just gotten her nose broke from that backhand. She said, "You were sleeping on my back porch." I apologized, put them in her car, and took them to the hospital, then I waited outside for three and a half hours until they got fixed up. I've had my jaw broke and it sucks.

I got her and the lil' one to tell me where that bully prick lived and worked. Of course he was gone when we got back. For two years he had been popping in and beating on them and taking money from her purse. I showed her how to bar her doors so they wouldn't open unless she removed the bar. I showed her a few other things to protect herself and the child.

Then I stalked that bully prick. I watched him be cruel to all beings he came into contact with—food truck lady, dogs, etc. Meanness, anger, and hatefulness had consumed his heart. After four days of seeing him being violently cruel every moment he was conscious, I was going to just let it go and catch a train until I heard him tell a man he could get some money. All he had to do was go slap the bitch and her f–in' kid and could empty her purse and her stash in the cabin, etc. I went back to her house and she let me in even though I was grungy, full beard, old army coat, and looking like the homeless mfkr I was. I told her to go to the back room with her lil' one because I was going to take care of the problem.

I made a sandwich and waited. Sure enough, here he came. He kicked the door in even though it wasn't locked. He saw me eating a pbj sandwich and drinking a beer and asked "Who the f– are you? You the SOB who knocked me out the other day?" I told him my name was Bum and I was going to get the job done and "Yeah, it was me who knocked you out the other day." I told him, "I should've killed you then, but I'm too soft-hearted. It wouldn't have been fair to kill you while you were knocked out."

He was a pretty good size, maybe 6'1" or 6'2" and weighing 200 pounds. I weighed about 130. He laughed and told me he was going to stomp me to death for interfering with a family matter. I was still eating the sandwich as he was running his mouth. I just knew he was going to jump over the kitchen island and think he was stomping on me. But when he came sailing over, I stuck an 8-inch butcher knife in him at the base of his sternum and angled it toward his heart, and not in a gentle way. He knew he was dying. He asked who I was—her brother or cousin or some shit. I said, "No, just a homeless bum on the run," but I'll not put up with the coward-ass BS he was doing, terrorizing a woman and lil' one. I told him he was getting some payback for all the mean-ass shit he had been pulling, beating on women and kids. Then I twisted the knife and killed him.

When I looked up, the lady and her lil' one were standing about three feet away. I apologized for killing the dude in their kitchen but it had to be done if they ever wanted to live in peace. The lil' one said, "Mister, you ain't done nothin wrong." They actually helped me carry him out to his car. I never told them my real name. If I hadn't of killed him, he would have killed one or both of them.

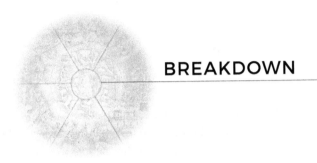

CHAPTER 13

BREAKDOWN

Even as Roy's physical health was beginning to break down, so were the bonds that held our group together. Starting in the spring of 2012, tension, anger, and broken trust threatened the integrity not only of our partnership, but of our practice.

Roy

Bro, you've pretty much convinced me you don't read my letters in their entirety. Like you don't start at the beginning and slowly read it word for word, line by line and THINK about what I'm saying or asking. I'm not saying that in anger, Bro, okay. I'm just slowly getting more and more assured that you have become convinced that I'm not too bright. Sure, you make a few comments about each letter, but you don't really put a lot of thinking time or much effort into trying to comprehend what I'm saying to you. I'm probably getting dumber with age.

Doug

You asked if I thought your letters were "empty and meaningless," you even used the word "stupid." If I thought your letters were "empty and meaningless," do you think I would spend 100s of dollars and lots of time turning them into a book or blog? You also asked if I watched TV while reading your letters. I don't have time to watch TV (though I do watch movies). I don't even listen to music. I'm going to take a little time to describe what else is going on, so you will better understand why I am sometimes late in responding to your letters including the one requesting money. [I was traveling to California for further testing of my prostate cancer and to Illinois to visit my mother who had gone into hospice.]

Roy

A good Christian friend of mine the other day even told me I was getting beside myself and when I asked him what he meant, he said it wouldn't make sense until I saw it for myself and now I see. I can only imagine what you all must have thought when I asked for even more f–ing money a couple of weeks ago. But instead of calling me on it like other people would have, saying "Look, you ungrateful f– you're not appreciating anything, just wanting more and more." No, instead your level of goodness of heart and love and kindness is so high that you dealt with my greed and ungratefulness with a kind and gentle "No." No harshness or foulness—the reactions of true Buddhists, ones who are sincere and understanding.

About a year after Roy and I resolved our differences, a new prisoner, Mike, became involved with the group. A young man, like Cody, Mike was serving a 38-year sentence for killing his father.

Roy

Another youngster is showing some interest in Buddhism. He's just finished *A Meditation Primer* so I sent *Awakening to the Sacred* to him. I've known him four years and really like him and he's a good kid who will share his last cup of coffee with you and will help anybody, no matter what color skin. He has a sharp mind and a good heart. He's pretty much in the same boat Cody was in before he met us. When he was 15 years old he shot and killed his father, who was a mean drunk and violent. His Mom died several years ago. Then he only had his Grandma left and she died a couple of years ago too.

Mike

One of the things Buddha said which I like most is that when Buddha became enlightened he said that anyone can become awake, enlightened, wise, unselfish, serene, and compassionate as the Buddha and that enlightenment is our birthright. I also like the teachings that lay out the progressive stages of insight. There are "fetters" which bind us to an unawakened state. I'm trying to work on getting rid of my "fetters," which are self-illusion, doubt, and skepticism and lust. Then I'll be Buddhafied!

I still don't know why, but a few weeks after Mike arrived on the scene, the friendship between the three men exploded. Mike and Cody seemed to gang up on Roy, taunting and picking on him. Roy responded by lashing out with verbal abuse in return, privately telling me that he was struggling with his own anger and suppressing the impulse to kill one or both of them.

Roy

I really felt like I've let you all down. I tried to be understanding with Cody and Mike because they're still "kids" and haven't gotten that playing business out of their systems, but man, when I feel like I wish someone would chop off my hands and just go ahead and give me a prosthetic, I sure as f–in' don't feel like playing some childish games, especially when Cody will purposefully aggravate and f– with me just to get me so angry that I'm ready to explode and then will say, "Oh, was just f–in' with ya, Dawg."

Bro, I've practically begged them both to stop playing, but to no avail. I don't know what to believe now from either one. They act serious as can be, then say, "Oh Dawg, was just playing." Bro, when you're hating the fact that you're alive because you feel so much pain, the last thing you want to do is play some kiddie game. ... So I've decided to quit talking with 'em.

I don't want to let this get in my heart as a killing anger because even as f–ed up as my body is, I'm still capable of a "heat of the moment" surge of adrenalin and combined with fury, that can make a person lose it, snap, which can make me capable of enhanced physical strength. Now, Bro, combine all that psychological stuff with knowing how to kill someone in a few different ways because you've been in a krazy life and you know you can slam a pencil into someone's neck in a few different places so that it would be up to "chance" if they survive. See where I'm coming from? Can you understand how I'm not into all this f–in' playing?

I'm completely through with Lil' Mike. His punk ass thought I was in the infirmary and went to running his mouth about his new "lick," his new score: You, Bro, is his new score. He went to talking about how if he writes the mfkr one time, he's got 'em. Talking about how he was sinking in his mfk hook and then he'd start getting a fat check.

Around the same time that his relationship with Cody and Mike was breaking down, Roy was struggling with the cognitive side effects of a new medication, which included disorientation and rage. A change in prescriptions eventually cleared his head.

Roy

I feel like a turd. I was so messed up in the brain. That's not the worst of it. F—ed up bad early today. I totally went ballistic, wishing death, miserable death on people. Cody and Lil' Mike are standing [nearby] trying to talk to me, telling me to "Let it Go," which seemed to infuriate me because I knew they were not feeling any of the pain I was screaming about in my hands and arms.

I have personally admitted out of my own f—in' mouth that I've been a real prick for going on five weeks now [because of the pain medication], but that doesn't seem to mean shit to the so-called Sangha Bros. I was told just a couple of hours ago that my pain "ain't nothing but an excuse." And Cody's perfect ass said that the doctor told him that there was nothing wrong with my neck. Bro, these two kids, who have all the use of their hands, legs, and feet, are suddenly the Perfect Buddhists who know all the answers.

In April of 2013, I wrote to reprimand Roy, Cody, and Mike about their behavior.

Doug

These past six weeks or so have been exceedingly difficult for Roy and Cody for health reasons. At this time of greatest difficulty was also the most intense time for mistreating each other. I understand how this can happen. But I want to remind you that our partnership is about letting go AND SPREADING KINDNESS. As far as I can tell, the way the three of you treated each other was BULLSHIT. Everyone has enough problems without you spreading poison rather than kindness. We all make mistakes, but I hope you will work VERY HARD to not make these kinds of mistakes in the future.

Letting go is about "Self."

Spreading kindness is about "US."

I hope to receive more letters that describe your practice of letting go and your practice of SPREADING KINDNESS.

Roy

I've already shook off the bullshit that went down with Mike, Cody, and me. I sent you the kite about what Mike said when he thought I wasn't here, and he swears that shit was exactly that—shit.... Ever since I called him on that foul ass shit—running game on you—he hasn't been trying to impress the other kids like that. Plus his behavior has changed in a positive way. And he has been putting some serious time in on studying the dharma—every day.

I'm just really feeling blessed to be able to help Cody and Mike as they begin to learn about Buddha's teachings.

Mike

Truth be told, if it wasn't for Buddha's teaching, I'd probably still be doing the same thing I was doing six weeks ago when Roy and I fell out. But instead, I've learned how to meditate and I've also learned how to transform my suffering (which probably caused Roy, Cody, and I to fall out) into joy and peace. And Bro, I'm discovering that one can turn all their anger, aggravation, hurt, and embarrassment, whatever it may be that's causing them to suffer, into joy and peace. It's a life saver in this place. Learning how to liberate myself from my suffering is a major turning point for me!

A few months after Roy, Cody, and Mike reconciled, I confronted what was to become the most serious breach of my trust. I had sent Cody some money to cover what he said were medical costs. It turned out he lied—there were no costs related to his surgery. I learned Cody had also lied at other times to get me to send him money. In all, I had sent him around $200 over several months. In August of 2013 I confronted him.

Doug

I talked to Ms. S. at the prison. She said you have spent all the money I sent you, on the 12th, 14th, and 19th. You had spent all the money when you told me you could not get access to the money because I deposited it in your phone account. Clearly you lied to me, which makes me sad. I understand why you did it. Now I have to wonder if you are interested in the practice only so that you can get money. That will not be an option anymore because I will not send you any money in the future, except $5 a month for postage beginning Jan 1, 2014, if you decide to continue writing.

I will continue to be pleased to write to you about your practice. I am NOT giving up on you. If you chose to not stay in touch, I will understand. The choice is up to you.

CHAPTER 14

THE FIFTH PARTNER

Our partnership consists of Roy, John, Tad, Cody, and myself—the fifth partner. It was founded on principles of equality, honesty, and Buddhist kindness. Although our lives and experiences and our relative "status," as perceived by the outside world, couldn't be more different, we truly considered ourselves peers. As a practitioner of Buddhism and meditation for more than 40 years, co-founder of the Eugene Buddhist Priory in 1973, and a lay minister in the Order of Buddhist Contemplatives, I often acted as a teacher in matters of Buddhism, and felt a teacher's sense of responsibility in encouraging the four men in their practice.

At the same time, I also felt very much their student. The ability of Roy, John, Tad, and Cody to emerge from lives of such tremendous suffering with such openness and grace humbles me. I am inspired daily by their ability and commitment to practice mindfulness and kindness in a place suffused with dehumanizing cruelty and lack of control over even the most basic aspects of their lives. Watching them struggle and fall in the face of extreme adversity, only to pull themselves back to their feet and recommit to their practice through sheer force of will, has caused me to take a hard look at the sincerity and resilience of my own practice, and challenged me to take my practice deeper than I could have ever imagined. They give me inspiration when I face my own adversity.

In my role of student, they would from time to time make suggestions or give advice that I would follow. In one case, Roy suggested that I send each partner a postcard while we traveled in Burma/Myanmar. To people on the outside with friends and family, receiving a postcard seems trivial. To those on the inside who almost never receive mail or visitors, receiving a postcard, especially one from a foreign country, and a Buddhist country at that, is far from trivial. In another instance, John advised me on how to counsel Roy while he was struggling with anger and pain.

John

Think about this Doug. I killed my own blood brother to protect my daughter and son. He [Roy] choked his father to death then sliced his mother's throat while she was in a back brace. We all pay for our wrongs in order to balance life out. Imagine his demons infesting his soul. He killed them when he was high and coming down, and they refused him money.

I know you get tired of hearing of his pain and his anger. Though he must let it out. You are a friend and teacher. What happens if there is no one to listen and no way to vent his hurt within? Understanding and compassion is the key. I use the words of Buddhism to help when he gets like that. He understands, but his punishment for absolution is greater than he can bear at this time. I remember we were there with you, suffering when you suffered through cancer, Linda's wreck, your mother's passing to another world, and your frustrations. I was proud to suffer with you. It helped me love life even more. When you suffer you learn and teach.

Listening to one another's advice and suggestions testified to our equality in the partnership and secured our responsibility to share our teaching with integrity, and from the heart. With honesty came trust. Over the years of our fellowship, Roy, John, Tad, Cody, and I have shared both our greatest strengths and our deepest vulnerabilities with one another, reaching out with kindness and support in times of need.

In addition to serving as teacher and partner, I also took on the role of an intermediary, coordinating discussion between the members of the group, maintaining connections between the partners when they were separated by the prison system, and in some cases helping my friends communicate with the outside world.

Roy, John, Tad, and Cody had formed friendships with one another when they met in prison and connected over their interest in Buddhism. However, like so many other aspects of prison life, staying in contact from day to day was out of their control. Being moved to a different cell, put in isolation, sent to the Hole, or transferred to a different prison meant they would be separated, with no way of communicating or even hearing news of one another—although they can write to the outside world, letters between prisoners are prohibited. Entering prison had ended most relationships these men had had in the outside world. Now I began to see how the vagaries of the prison system meant that any friendships formed on the "inside" would inevitably be taken from them as well. Sometimes transfers happen so suddenly that prisoners are unable to say good-bye to a friend of ten years, never to hear from him again.

Along with sharing Buddhist books and teachings, I would often share news with the men about how their friends were doing. I forwarded greetings received and passed along updates on their health and well-being, and facilitated group discussions about the principles we were studying. When one of the men shared a new insight into his practice, I sent copies to the rest of the group. Sometimes I added my comments and feedback or shared insights and experiences of my own.

Doug

Dear Roy, John, Tad, and Cody,

I went to hear the Dalai Lama speak. What I want to emphasize were these words of his: "Prayer and meditating are not enough. We must ACT." I realized why my mantra had become "loving-kindness." I am to transform my mindfulness practice into a mindful loving-kindness practice. My mindfulness has the intent of helping all living things, beyond reducing my suffering and giving me moments of peace and joy. It is basically the same as this half of our partnership: "spreading kindness."

Do the words of the Dalai Lama and the idea of a mindful, loving-kindness practice encourage you to put even more emphasis on spreading kindness to the people, frogs, and crickets, you come in contact with?

Do we now have an even sharper focus for our partnership? THE PURPOSE OF LETTING GO IS TO ALLOW US TO DO A BETTER JOB OF SPREADING KINDNESS. As Keizan [Jiyu-Kennett] said, "Treat both your body and mind with care. Every day is a good day. Everyone is the vessel of the truth." Everyone is part of our practice.

The only question is whether we recognize it or not. I would like to hear your thoughts about this. The implications are radical.

In the spirit of honesty as a foundation of our partnership, I also shared my own struggles, both with my practice and in my life. When I was diagnosed with cancer, helped care for my mother through her illness and death, coped with debilitating injury and chronic pain, and struggled with a year-and-a-half depression, Roy, John, Tad, and Cody were among the inner circle of friends with whom I discussed the intimate details.

Doug

I'm having a bit of a health problem, nothing like Roy though.

It started about 10 at night, Vesak eve [a Buddhist festival]. My urine was bright red. 45 minutes later it is bright red along with lumps that I first felt pass through my urethra, then saw drop into the toilet bowl. I was horrified, having no idea what might have set off this discharge. Had my prostate cancer turned aggressive? A little after midnight, I lay down and felt pain shoot out from the end of the bottom rib on my left side of my back. Was I returning to the beginning of another two years of back pain, sleeplessness, and forced inactivity leading to depression? The pain kept me awake in all positions, on my back, on my left side, and on my right side. Relentlessly the night bore on. My fear intensified. Directing my attention to my breathing did not diminish the fear that my life could be turning into an on-going struggle with pain and discomfort or worse. I faced the fact that when life is relatively easy, my practice is relatively easy. Just the opposite when fear overtakes me.

About 2:40 a.m. I took more painkillers and a sleeping pill. Recognizing how quickly my practice was taken over by fear, I was humbled by the fragility of my practices of mindfulness, meditation, and loving-kindness. I switched my mantra to saying, "mindfulness, meditation, loving-kindness." I decided that the next day I would no longer put off the calls to the three elderly widows I occasionally visit and talk to (my aunt Pat, my first Tai Chi teacher's widow, and my devoted now-retired secretary of a dozen years.)

Sleep came about 4 a.m. I get out of bed at 6 a.m. I'm hungry. I fix cereal with fruit and protein powder and tea. I go to Vesak.

Over the years, one of the ways I supported our partnership was with material and financial support. They often ask for new books on Buddhism, sometimes specifying a title. By now I've sent nearly 200 books, many donated by the Eugene Buddhist Priory. In addition to Buddhist books, I've also sent along educational books on writing, art, and other topics, as well as books they request to give as gifts to other prisoners and occasionally a guard. These books range from word puzzles to world almanacs.

I send the partners money for hygiene (deodorant and soap) and food as well as to support their acts of kindness within the prison. Roy, John, Tad, and Cody share the food they buy with others, and often look for particular items that might bring happiness to another prisoner or make that person's life easier—things as simple as shoes or a radio. With the money I have sent they can buy goods at the prison commissary to give or trade for the needed items. From time to time, I'd worry that our partnership was really about me sending money. I would think back to what Roy wrote about Mike, "…running his mouth about his new 'lick,' his new score: You." And there were Cody's lies to get money out of me. While my trust seldom falters, I do not send money to the new men who have joined the partnership.

I also sometimes intervened for the men in the outside world. For Cody, I would contact his daughter's relatives to see how his daughter Blossom was faring. I wrote John's daughter about his practice as a way of encouraging her to visit him. Many of the men would ask me to call relatives of other prisoners, to ask about their health or if they would write or call. To help Tad qualify for parole, I made several searches and phone calls to find a sex counselor who would agree to see him, write a letter stating that commitment, and send it to the parole board. His plan after parole was to live with his grandmother while he got on his feet.

Doug

Dear Tad,

I talked to your Grandmother. She said she is not doing well and that she loves you so much. You were so little when she brought you home from the hospital that is why she nicknamed you Tadpole. She said she got a picture of me from you; she liked being able to see who I am. She sounded good.

. . . .

I called your Grandmother as soon as I read your letter. Yesterday your Grandmother was looking at the teddy bear you sent and started crying. She is so happy now to hear about the news [that you can be paroled before too long]. I am to tell you that she loves you very, very much.

Both Tad and I became alarmed when his grandmother abruptly stopped responding to my phone calls. After several unsuccessful attempts, I wrote to his niece.

Tad wrote me that he is very worried about his Grandmother. I just now opened his letter and called his Grandmother. The number is not working. Can you write Tad soon and tell him what has happened to his Grandmother. In addition for his concern for her health, he will not be able to be paroled because he was going to live with his Grandmother, which no longer seems possible, at least at this time.

A Spiritual Mentor

While I tried to help Roy, John, Tad, and Cody improve their lives in prison, the most important way I have supported them has been by encouraging their practice, offering guidance where it was needed, and answering their questions about Buddhism and meditation.

Cody

I'm about to look more into my inner self and look into what makes me think what I do or why I talk to the others guys sometimes and just plain out lie. I made up a long story the other day, just straight up lied. Why? I'm here to spread kindness and compassion, Bro, so tomorrow when the guy wakes up I'm going to tell him Hey, Bro, I lied for no reason. I just wanted to be what? Cool? Wanted a part of something? I don't know, Doug, but I got to look into these gray areas I got going on because I'm taking this all to heart because I want to help, not hurt. Encourage, not impress. These are my Brothers, Bro, and if I can't keep the natural Cody and present myself, not some made up story or fantasy story about something, then I need to step back and realize what is going on here.

Doug

I am very familiar with wanting to be special, to impress or at least to please people. So I understand why you lied to the person to impress him. My lies usually come from wanting to please the other person. So instead of saying I don't want to go for a walk, I will say that I have a conflict. Being aware of telling the lie is motivating me to stop lying. Your awareness indicates you are now motivated to stop lying.

. . . .

Roy

There is nothing as Frightening as Ignorance & Stupidity in action and, too often, I find me so active with Stupidity & Ignorance.

Doug

You talk about your stupidity and ignorance. I have learned that everything is Buddha nature, our inherent tendency toward the good, to be kind; so when we act in ways that disappoint us, we are still Buddha nature. Getting back on the path means we are not disappointed so often. Being disappointed is part of our Buddha nature too.

. . . .

Roy

In looking after oneself, one looks after others. And looking after others, one looks after oneself.

Doug

In deep meditation one IS others and others IS one.

. . . .

Cody

I want to talk to you and see if you mind if I call you Dad and Mrs. Linda Mom because lately in my feelings you are the family that I wish I was grown up by. I know you and Mrs. Linda have two wonderful women [our daughters]. Can I be you and Mrs. Linda's adopted son? I feel a good energy of love from y'all like I'm a son to you. I really miss my family and would love to be a son to you and Mrs. Linda. Will you please talk to each other about it?

Doug

Linda and I are very touched by your asking if you can refer to us as Mom and Dad. One other time our daughters asked us to informally adopt a friend of theirs. It did not work out well. So for the time being, let's continue as partners and continue to teach each other about mindfulness and kindness.

. . . .

Cody

I'm reading [your book on mindfulness and kindness, *How Love Wins*] out loud to the guy next door in hopes that not only is he listening, but some of the other guys around me listen and hear me as well. If they hear the wonderful teachings that you put in this book, they are going to find life a lot better because I have and still am learning. He is a really good fella, full of kindness and compassion and really smart and really is helping me out with a lot of problems I did not realize [I had]. He gets a check every month. Well, when he ran out of money, I noticed how he did not talk much and was down. Then he got a letter in the other day saying he had $200.00 on the way and the first thing he did was holler, "Hey Cody, I got my money in Bro." I said, "That's cool, Bro." He said, "Now I can pay you back that bag of coffee." I told him, "Nah, man, I'm good." Then I asked him if I could talk to him and share something with him and he said, "Yeah, Bro, what's up?" I said, "Man, you get all this money and spend it all on pills and don't have none left for coffee or stuff that matters." I told him that when he runs out and ain't got pills, it becomes a suffering for him when he said he got money for the pills, he seems happy. I asked him, "Now in two weeks, this joy you have now, will you have it then?"

I realized a lesson with the conversation. I said, "Bro, my mind has been on looking forward to my birthday on March 8 because my buddy said we could see about him sending me some money for my B-Day for songs on my mp4 player." He said, "What's the problem with that? It's your birthday." I said, "Well, Bro, I expect this to happen kind of like a lust." He said, "Yeah, but it's your birthday man." I said, "It is not that. The problem is that I have not been focused on NOW. My mind is on something in the future."

Doug, I'm explaining this because I'm taking this serious and want to really better my life, but let me finish what I'm saying. I got so distracted that all I could think about was songs, songs I would love to have and listen to. I went through my pre-order on my mp4 and ordered 80 songs at $2.00 a song. That would be $160.00. Now this was wrong and I realized I need to fix it because that old greed was coming out of me and that is not the new Cody no more. I had my mind on 80 new songs and greed for all of them songs was thinking of something in the future instead of what I need now. I just wanted to be honest and share that with you Doug. I got really upset with myself because you have really taught me better, but I did learn something from this and would like feedback on this.

Doug

What you said to your neighbor with the pill problem and how you then saw you had the same problem only with songs, which is much less serious of course—but as you point out it is VERY IMPORTANT TO LET ALL GREED GO, including greed for songs. Your explanation was clear and thorough. Thank you.

. . . .

As a devout Buddhist, Roy is a vegetarian. However, because meals in prison are heavily based around meat and animal protein, he was losing weight. As his friend, I urged him to do what was necessary to take care of his body.

Doug

I just got your most recent letter. Are you in the Hole for saving the cricket? You are amazing. I respect you for your integrity.

Kanzeon (Japanese) or Kuan Yin (Chinese) is the bodhisattva of compassion. She has a thousand arms to help those suffering in the world. One of those arms of compassion is for herself. Each person must decide how to be compassionate toward himself/herself. The founder of our lineage was a woman with diabetes—she was told she needed to eat meat for her health and she ate meat. The Dalai Lama eats meat. They decided they needed to take care of their health; they know there will be consequences, and they accept them. You are a noble and principled person. Your work as a bodhisattva of compassion will be hindered by poor health. Eating tuna and staying out of the Hole would improve your health. What you do with it is up to you, balancing your high standards of integrity and bodhisattva vow of compassion. (I am not a brave person; I would not have stopped the guard from killing the cricket. I accept that about myself and train as best I can.)

. . . .

Roy

Have you ever come off "cross" at someone, when later on when you looked at it you were like, "Where did that come from?"

Doug

Yes. I am gradually getting better at recognizing when I am being cross at even a slight level and when my speech is not "right speech." Last night we meditated with a couple. He had an eye injury that was well healed. He said it had changed from abnormal to normal. Trying to make a joke, I said, "Do you think it will make the rest of your face normal?" Although intended as a joke, it also is speaking negatively about his face. Not helpful on my part. I also realized (again) that once I do something, I couldn't go back and undo it.

. . . .

I also counseled Roy on his anger toward the prison system because of its cruelty. I noticed that, although he had largely succeeded in responding to guards, nurses, and other individuals with kindness and compassion, he seemed to be harboring a deep anger toward the medical system and the doctors. In the summer of 2014, I wrote two letters to challenge him to reflect on how his anger was affecting him, those around him, and his mindful kindness practice.

Doug

Have you thought about how the anger you feel toward ADC [Arkansas Department of Corrections] affects you? How would it be if their harmful acts brought, on the feeling side, a "Nuttin' 2it" and "focus on others in some kind of way?" As I said, there's no question about your anger being justified. The question is what is best for your training, because what is best for your training is, I think, also good for letting go and sharing kindness.

. . . .

Point 1. You assume that [the doctor] knows how to make you better and is refusing to do so. She is doing that because she does not like you? She liked Cody, which is why the state spent thousands of dollars to treat his brain tumor and do surgery?

Richard, who wrote you, had damaged nerves and pain that would knock him to the ground when he walked. He had insurance and money. They could not fix his pain.

My mom had unstoppable pain. She had money and insurance.

Point 2. Is it skillful means to assume that [the doctor] and the medical staff are intentionally withholding treatment? Is this ASSUMPTION [that the doctors want to harm you] helping you inspire others to follow the Buddha?

Point 3. Is there a way to express your unimaginable pain other than through anger?

I wish with all my heart that your koan [puzzle for contemplation] were not unimaginable pain. I hope I NEVER have that koan. I am so sorry that unimaginable pain is your koan. BUT IT IS YOUR KOAN.

Throughout our relationship, Roy and I wrote to each other often about Buddhism, mindfulness, and the transformative power of kindness. And yet, at the same time, his body was slowly breaking down. As his disability progressed, I sent him books about pain management, put him in contact with teachers and practitioners who had trained for many years with intense pain, and finally sent him two books on grief—for the loss of the use of his body and for the loss of a life without pain. After reading these books, we had one of our rare phone conversations in which he told me how he was finally coming to terms with these losses and turning away from anger. (Later Roy would lose the use of his hands and was not able to write; from that time on, we could stay in touch only by phone.)

During that call he told me that looking at his anger as part of the grieving process had given him a new perspective. Having read Healing After Loss: Daily Meditations For Working Through Grief, *he shared two statements that struck him deeply: "When in deep melancholy, act with kindness toward another. The medicine for suffering is a healing friend." He went on to tell me that he realized his path must be one of courage to get above his pain and to be able to act with kindness. He said, "I was getting caught up in me instead of thinking of the suffering of others."*

During the entire 20-minute call he did not once speak of his anger or even of his pain. And I was humbled to hear about how he was still practicing kindness. He spoke of how he had given a ballpoint pen to a prisoner who loves to write, and how the man responded with as much gratitude as if he had handed him a $50 bill. A guard who was usually surly and negative surprised Roy, who had been discussing Buddhism with him for some time, by smiling and greeting him in the morning for the first time.

He also struck up a friendship with one of the nurses in the infirmary. "The new nurse is compassionate and cheerful. I told her how much I appreciated her working here because there is a shortage of nurses and she could work anywhere she wanted. The third time I saw her, I told her the third time how much I appreciated her working here. She looked at me and finally said, 'You're serious aren't you?'"

But most of all, Roy was moved by the actions of the nurse who had resigned in protest over his treatment, and told me about how he had walked all the way back to his barracks with tears in his eyes, thinking, "Someone stood up and gave up their job for someone like me."

PART IV

TRANSCENDENCE

CHAPTER 15

BACK ON THE PATH

Roy's darkest time brought him to thoughts of suicide, but he reached out to me each time he got close. Feeling helpless and discouraged, I told him we would continue to discuss our practice. But I would not advise him about suicide. I have given two funeral eulogies and both were for people who had died by suicide. I am not competent to speak of life and death to those in deep darkness.

Even as he suffered, Roy's practice brought him back to the path of kindness, mindfulness, and Buddhism. He walked this path still carrying the burden of his crimes, and now also the burden of debilitating chronic pain.

Roy

Your loving-kindness, compassion, understanding and wisdom, and invaluable teachings have been what's brought me through the last eight months. I was "close" a couple times to getting the "stuff" needed to OD, but each time I was dangerously close to "doing the deed," you picked up the phone and accepted the collect call that was costing some major pesos. You listened to me cry, whine, and complain. Then, with a calmness in your voice, you spoke with wisdom, kindness, and compassion. I felt all that and so much more in your voice and once Miss Linda even said a few words and I could feel her Loving-kindness in her voice, which was calm and full of "I care about you." That love kept me from "doing the deed." I just couldn't OD with knowing how incredibly much you all have done to help me and show me you care. Even though I've already run your phone bill up at least $150 more than it should be, you still accepted my call. When most would have said, "F– this" and refused, you still remained my rock. You really were a lifeline and a life preserver thrown to me when I fell overboard.

. . . .

And Bro, ask your Buddhist friend [a Buddhist contemplative], if you don't mind, why it is that when my pain is almost at a level to drive me insane, when I'm using my mala beads or just pinpointing my focus on those three pictures here by my side and y'alls and my extended dharma family's loving-kindness and compassion, that I get a short Wow!—clear, Buddha-ful, Blissful moments where I see where I'm not looking at things right. Where I get insight into where I'm "off course." I mean, I finally saw that I've been trying to get away from my body and when I accepted my body and all the dents and dings and frame damage and shit that come with it, I felt a pressure release.

. . . .

I've started my own "physical therapy" workout. It hurts like hell, but I can already feel a difference. I'm using a towel to work resistance against resistance and have managed to roll up a sock, which I squeeze in different ways to work out muscles and get some use of my hands. It still pisses me off that they are using the bullshit excuse of scar tissue to keep me from [getting] surgery and fixing my hands and wrist.

Finally realized I'm going to have to break free from the prison of depression. I finally realized that I had given up on life. I wasn't even washing my face when I woke up, but the dark, black cloud of depression had me living, no, just existing, in a world of darkness. I can see now, though. I've been doing the exercises and cleaning my cell and getting back to the old me.

In the last week and one half I've only walked to the shower once because of the walking involved. I took a shower today and the walk wasn't as bad as I feared. I faced the fear and walked. Well, me and Buddha and all my dharma family walked there "together."

. . . .

I just got back from the infirmary where I've been since 8 a.m. It seems I knocked myself out when I hit the top of my forehead on the corner of my table. I woke up with guards all in my cell and nurses trying to get to me. Right now I look like the Elephant Man or the kid in Mask. I can barely see out of my left eye because it is so swollen. The right one is swollen a little. My forehead is swollen so much it protrudes beyond my eyebrows. It scares me to look at myself in the mirror, but, in a way it doesn't scare me. I can't really explain it, but if I don't wake up here in the morning, I know I've come a long way from the Roy who didn't know anything about Buddhism and have really made some progress since coming to know you and your Buddha-ful, Beautiful family.

········

I'm not going to stop sitting. Ain't going to stop my practice. Damn it, I'm trying to sit even more. I'm trying to "sit" standing up against the wall, hands in a mudra position. I'm not trying to resist anything, just trying to go with it, with everything. I've lost two pounds but think that's just due to the energy getting used or stress.

········

I've been meditating a lot lately because the pain from this nerve damage has been red lining almost 24/7. No way was I aware Sgt. Eason was there. I was still in Limbo with meditation, still "in," when I became aware she was at my cell door because of the perfume they apply by the pint it seems, but I still hadn't opened my eyes. She said, "Tester, is you breathing when you do that meditation because I can't tell if you breathing." "Yeah, Sarge, I'm breathing but just real shallow. The deeper I get the less breathing I do." Then she asked, "How many times a week you do it?" I told her every day, at least twice a day, sometimes three and four times a day, and at least twenty minutes at a time, but usually a half hour or more. I told her the longer I meditate, the deeper I get. She said, "Well, shit, then what?" I said I try to get deep enough so I am you and you are me and we're no longer two but one energy, one with everyone and everything. She laughed and said, "Okay, okay, that's enough Buddha for me for today. Here, them nice peoples [Doug] wrote you a thick-ass letter."

········

Well, I didn't have too hectic a day in Paradise. I spent most of today reading in two different magazines and reading about the dharma. It's a good way to spend time. Read, then sit for 20–25 minutes, move around, do some pulling and resisting exercises, drink one-half bottle of water, then sit. What a way to spend the day that Free-world folks have to pay out some fees to do while

I'm groovin' on Buddhism 18 hours or 18 minutes. My schedule is flexible. I can sit first, then read, and fit in some walking meditation. No problem. Paradise, Bro. I got so many teachers and my every waking hour has me having access to them and I only need raise my voice and teachers struggle to see who gets to interact with me so I can deepen and strengthen my practice through "hands-on training."

....

I've come to realize I must work harder at not becoming attached to the thought, the desire for less pain. I've been working on this for close to a week, just lettin' the pain be there, kind of like making room in the cab of a pickup truck for your dog or another person (hitchhiker). I've been working on making room for the pain.

....

Today, well, this evening when I ended my meditation, my pain "felt" different. It's hard to explain. The pain is still there in all its ugliness, but it's like when there is a lot of noise from a chainsaw. You've gotten out of your truck and realize how serious the noise is so you put in a pair of earplugs and the noise loses its sharpness and is more acceptable to the point where you're not "distracted" by it. That's how my pain is right now.

....

This is one of those rare quiet times in the block. The guys just got through watching some DVD movies and now that they are over and the TV is off, no one is hollering or being loud and rude. It's a precious time. While I was meditating the silence became so loud it broke through my Letting Go. Have you ever experienced being in the "Zone"—that beautiful, still, empty place where there's nothing f–ing up the preciousness of awareness? You feel like you're shimmering within in a shimmering existence; it's like looking across the Salt Flats in Utah in the blazing heat and seeing the heat waves and the way they don't really have any form. Then poof, you're back in the moment and you see solid forms. You're back to reality, but reality is easier to deal with ever since I've experienced that special place of stillness with the heat waves. Because of that, my life in prison stopped being miserable; it didn't matter any longer that I'd never be physically free again.

....

A couple of years back you sent me a couple of books written by Boowa Bhikkhu and there were a couple more books on Theravada traditions. Right before I got locked down I wrote to you about experiencing the Heat Monkeys [heat waves]; it was like looking down a Hot Ass Highway, seeing all that shimmering, vibrating energy field a time or two because of an extended meditation, as though I were spiraling inward and coasting to a perfect stop, like on top of a pinpoint or razor's edge. Balanced. My experiences never last more than a few minutes, then it's like I just "open my eyes" and feel purity and total koolness through my senses.

. . . .

When I read a few pages in Boowa Bikkhu's Path of Arhatship, it caused me to shudder and my whole body shimmered and buzzed because what he described is how the hell I experience what I did but did not know what it was. I ain't really knowing how to explain this. I didn't know what was doing what, though. For years I've had a running tape of Buddha, Buddha, Buddha, but have never known that other cats did. I just did it to try to distract my mind from thinking or saying stupid shit. Boowa is the only person who says what I was experiencing. Kool. Forrest Gump. Shit happens.

. . . .

When I told you about listening to the silence while meditating, I had no idea that others were into the same groove. It blew me away when I saw an article in one of my Buddhist magazines about listening to the silence. The way the monk described it made me kind of spooked. When I finished the article I felt WOW. There was some joy in me that was grooving like a Thai forest monk who had been in the forest doing sitting and walking meditation three times a day for mucho years. But just the thought that I'm grooving the same kind of groove of some Thai forest monks is assurance I wasn't doing something wrong.

. . . .

I woke up this morning to excruciating pain in my feet from the tips of the three middle toes to about three inches up to the top of each foot. The balls of both feet were pulsing with explosions of intense pain. My mind started to amplify the pain by focusing only on the pain. I was instantly fighting and resisting the pain. Then I looked up to see [the photo of] the Buddha statue in your backyard and the picture of the sunrise coming alive over Angkor Wat and I realized I was practically holding my breath.

Ah! Breathing! Yeah, breathe, easy and softly. Get this breathing under control, slow it down, let it flow, just let it be. I sat up straight as possible to "open up" and kept my eyes on those three pictures, then started softly reciting prayers and mantras and pictured them gently wrapping around the nerves in my feet, which were the cause of all this unkoolness. As I softly gazed at those pictures I felt I was somehow connecting with all the compassion and loving-kindness and positive energy coming from you all and all the dharma family [those who follow the teachings of the Buddha] you have connected me with. It was like I could feel everyone sending merit and Buddha-ful thoughts and energy.

I directed all this "dharma-medicine" to the pain and just stayed with this "groove," not fighting, but embracing the pain with tenderness and compassion. I was so into this "groove" that the guard had to yell to get my attention. He said, "What the f– is wrong with you? You doped up?" And he was a bit hateful about it, but all I could do was feel compassion for him because of all the verbal abuse from so many ignorant—product of their environment—fellow prisoners. He isn't normally like this and usually talks to me in a polite way, so I knew he was being verbally assaulted in a major way.

The more I focused on sending him merit and kind thoughts, the less I was affected by my pain. When I pointed at my feet, he said, "F–! Tester, I'm so sorry man." I told him it was okay. Even though I was able to reduce the pain through this "dharma medicine," they still took me to the infirmary. I couldn't stand on my feet, Bro. The doctor said I was lucky to have gone eight years without this happening already. I had already realized that myself. Back in my cell I spent about two hours meditating and gently but repeatedly applying this oh so Buddha-ful dharma-medicine.

. . . .

I see and feel ya'alls love, Bro, and it's like a swimmer who has gotten too far out or someone who has fallen overboard and has been swimming until they're close to giving up, then they get a glimpse of the shore far in the distance and it gives them renewed strength. Those times when I've been hurting so intensely are also the times when I've been wrapped up in self, as if I'm the only person alive experiencing such ugly pain. When I think of all those people out there who have it so much worse than me, my pain just ever so slightly lessens.

. . . .

It's midnight. The tiny spider is also a teacher of the present. He abseils [rappels] and then just is. Total awareness. Sometimes he will just hang above my head. I feel such a spiritual connection with this tiny creature. He, or rather it, will hang or sit in awareness. Whenever I see it abseil and do nothing but be, I'll meditate. Such patience.

Reconciliation

Roy seldom had contact with his only sister after he went to prison. A devout Christian, she distanced herself after he converted to Buddhism.

You should have seen her face when I said there are a lot of similarities in Buddhism and Christianity, like "love thy neighbor as thyself" and "thou shalt not kill" and "do unto others as you would have them do unto you." The more I showed her what we had in common, the more horrified her expression got. It was like her expression was saying, "Get thee behind me Satan!" A lot of what Buddha taught is identical to what Jesus taught and that is a fact. I mean, "Thou shalt not kill" means the same regardless who says it.

Two years later, Roy received a rare letter from his sister.

My little nephew Christopher and my sister wrote. I was overwhelmed with a great joy at getting another chance to reconnect with family. Lil' Christopher wrote a short letter that stroked my heart with "genuine" love. He says, "Thanks for the letters and the pictures. I am sorry I haven't written back in a long time. I just keep forgetting and putting it off"—like kids are apt to do and big kids. me—"Could you please send a picture of football people? I'm playing this year. My number is 41. We had a jamboree Saturday and I caught an interception. I hope I can see you in Heaven."

Had me smiling and wiping a few happy tears. Very, very Kool Happening. Then, my sister wrote: "Christopher wrote you a letter and you'll get it with this one. I believe this was maybe the result of a discussion in Sunday School. I didn't ask the reason, though. He has asked for a football drawing, not knowing things like this cost money so I'm sending you some money. I hope your health has improved or at the least, the pain is manageable. Donna."

You all should have seen the happy tears and big smile those two letters generated. The guard gave me only one letter at first, which was my nephew's, and I was reading those well written, neatly printed words of his when the guard stepped back into my cell to give me the one from my sister. I couldn't read her letter for a couple minutes because the tears of joy flowed when I read, "I hope I see you in Heaven." They flowed. He seemed so much more grown up than his age, so mature. Then reading my sister's letter with her saying she felt humbled from the teaching she received from his reaching out to me with "a Love that Christ would have smiled at." She said she didn't question his reason when he said he wanted to write to me because it was obvious Christ was using a child.

Ordained

After years of studying Buddhism and practicing its principles, Roy asked to formally become a Buddhist. The ceremony, analogous to a Christian baptism, centers on making a commitment to follow the moral teachings of Buddhism. In my Zen tradition, the ceremony, called Jukai, is a week-long retreat held at a monastery. On January 20, 2015, Rev. Leon Kackman, a monk in the Order of Buddhist Contemplatives, and now prior of the Portland Buddhist Priory in Oregon came to Arkansas to perform a shortened version of the Jukai ceremony, formalizing Roy's conversion to Buddhism.

Gassho Bro. Beautiful experience that was powerful enough to almost completely overshadow my pain. Very loving warmth enveloped. I was in the infirmary and had just got my IV out an hour before, so it was easier to do a kind of modified bow. Some real coolness radiated and shined in Rev. Leon's eyes and smile. I thank you for all y'alls help because I know you and Miss Linda played a big part in making this Beautiful Happening.

I was sitting at 5 a.m. and visualizing the ceremony when I realized what Rev. Leon said at one point. We were talking about spreading loving-kindness and joy with everyone, not just certain few. He said, "and now that you've reached 'your final days,' it is very important to sow as much loving kindness and joy as possible."

[There is] a peace within my heart that began to glow when I accepted that my impermanence is fast approaching and in fact could happen at any moment. Gonna spend the time doing my best to live up to the Code of Integrity of the Boddhisattva.

I am making arrangements to have my papers sent to y'all when I cross over. I told Leah I'd like for y'all to go through my paperwork, kind of getting a glimpse of me. Check out my notes, poems, mantras, etc. After y'all have checked out all my papers, for y'all to remember me by, then burn all the paperwork y'all don't keep then spread the ashes in y'all's acres of forest. Maybe on a bluff where eagles nest or near a wolf den. Some such place. I'll be there Bro, in spirit. Think you and Miss Linda can do that for me? With my Sister Leah Jo joining in the ceremony? Will write a letter to y'all that can be read out loud. Is this request Kool with y'all?

CHAPTER 16

PLANTING SEEDS

John

You ever get to the place in life where you feel you just hit a rut? I hit that spot long ago. It got to the point where I said if this is it, just let me pass in my sleep. I don't even want to wake up if life holds nothing more for me. I wanted some kind of sign. Something that would show me I had more to give. If not, I didn't want to go on. I would not commit suicide; I just didn't have nothing left.

And I got that sign from the very moment of my waking, the other morning, all day. First I read this passage in *Our Daily Bread*:

> *We may face some limiting circumstances today. Whether it is the result of our failure, or through no fault of our own, we can go through it or seek God's strength to "grow" through it. The challenge of every confinement is to increase rather than decrease: to grow and not diminish. The Lord's goal is to give us a future and a hope.*

In my Dhammapada, [a collection of Buddha's teachings], I opened to The World, page 169, and read:

> *Live your life well*
> *In accord with The Way*
> *Avoid a life of distraction.*
> *A life well-lived leads to contentment,*
> *Both now and in the future.*

Later in the day I snatched up *The Heart of Buddha's Teaching*, [by Thich Nhat Hanh] and I just opened it up. Not to anything in particular, but just to read. And there my last sign was: Chapter 13, Right Action [Behaving in a skillful and ethical manner]. So I ask you, what more an answer could I have received when I reached out for one?

. . . .

Like Roy, after years of study, John asked to formally become a Buddhist. Rev. Leon Kackman performed a shortened version of the Jukai ceremony on January 20, 2015.

They came and got me out of solitary confinement and placed me in the holding cell for attorney visits. I waited for about forty minutes and Leon came in the other side of the glass. He was nothing like I expected. We talked about different things related to practice and hindrances of practices.

He proceeded to take me through the ceremony. Though I was scared of messing up, and I did a few times, I really enjoyed it. It was a release within. Then the idea that I am placed on record with 2,600 years plus of Great Masters was overwhelming. The ceremony was not what it could have been because the Chaplain hates Buddhists. So we didn't get the water or incense. We did have a miniature Buddha statue. Cool. All in all I enjoyed it very much. Coming back though, the Chaplain got in my face, being asinine about the whole thing, taunting me. He won't let us have our Rakusu [a bib-like garment that symbolizes formally being a Buddhist], because he said it could be made into a rope to hang ourselves. Yet the Muslims get a prayer rug that could be unbraided and made into a 20-foot rope. He really dislikes me and Roy bringing Buddhism into the Unit. He tried to get my ire up and it did for about thirty minutes, then I forgave him and sent blessings of healing to him to his mind and heart.

. . . .

I am just so elated to be alive and to help those who are lost when I can. They are fuel for my flame and I'm a flame in the dark for them. So in all, we all need each other, not just here, but in the entire world.

. . . .

I had a few guards talking to me the other day and they agreed on one thing. They said, "Bruno, you walk around the prison, or you're locked down [in the Hole], and you've always got a smile on your face. You laugh and joke all the time. How can you do that?" I looked up and smiled, then said, "I'm crazy!" They laughed. I said, "No, this is only a place and as with a school, a house, or even a ship, the body is not confined, for you can still move and the mind is free to think about anything. The heart is free to love and the soul is the pure essence of it all."

· · · · · · · ·

While meditating, the strangest thing happened. I was sitting cross-legged on my bunk and staring out my door through the bars. When I closed my eyes, the image of the bars stayed on my retinas. We've all been through this, but this is what dawned on me. As humans we have metaphorically symbolized light and dark for good and bad, God and Devil. Why is it that while looking at the light we see the dark, and yet when we close our eyes, the opposite happens? The light becomes dark and the dark light. While practicing Zen or whatever we do to enlighten ourselves, we push the darkness from us and allow the light, but the dark must go somewhere else, whether out into the world or within ourselves. It never truly abates; it just moves somewhere else.

Earlier in his life, John had attacked two men who had been harassing an elderly couple in a trailer park. As a result of the assault, he ended up getting arrested, lost his job, and saw his marriage fall apart. I asked him if he would have handled things differently today.

At that age I "was" a drug addict, alcoholic, swinger/wife swapper, and a criminal. We would have to change all of that to answer the question. Yet, let's assume that I was like I am now. I would have handled the situation totally different. Except, "if" I was, back then, like I am now, I would never have been in that state nor even married to the woman I was married to. Or would I?

We could speculate on many things to an infinitude of endings or outcomes. The possibilities are unimaginable. But, to what end? When searching for the "what ifs" in life, you cloud the mind of "what is."

Let's say, for instance, "what if" you [Doug] had excelled in athletics and completed academics with only the passing GPA needed to stay in athletics? Take into consideration you were not into Buddhism at the time. So by all actuality, how would your life have turned out? Would you still have met and married your wonderful and beautiful wife? Would we have ever met? It is the "what is" that has brought us all to the point and place we are today. It is the effects of the "what is" that has determined the definition of who we are here and now.

Yes, the "What ifs" will delude the mind, eluding reality and thereby incurring false pretensions upon our thoughts. This in turn creates a mental and emotional wall between our goal to enlightenment, the truth.

Do not look back and conclude that "What if" I had not done this another way. It no longer matters. So don't dwell upon something that is not. Concentrate on what is, and move forward from that point. We must deal with what we have now. This is all we can change, nothing else. Do this and you will free your mind of doubt.

· · · · · · · ·

I wish I could have met you when I was a scared kid on the streets, needing love instead of hate. Though if it had happened, I would not have learned that the meaning of suffering is to help others feel love, compassion, and hope within themselves. Life not only taught me how to suffer, but nature was a protective cocoon. True suffering is about those who deny the love within themselves. I once suffered like that.

· · · · · · · ·

I see so much tragedy out in the world it hurts my heart knowing "I" once was one of those who did the evil of some things. I am so glad I met with you and your family, Doug. You have helped turn my life around. I never cared for anyone before, not even myself. Now I want to reach out to all I can and share my life and give my opinion on options that would help change one's thinking, thus changing a habit formed over time, regardless if it's hereditary or learned. Whether I see the effects or not, I know the seeds will have been planted; where one seed may die, another will grow, bear fruit and plant seeds themselves. The same as you have done, and are still doing. In all, it is both giving and receiving, not only from you, but others. You see the beauty of it and you teach and learn in turn. Almost like a mathematical equation and amazing that everything comes in pairs—together, yet apart.

So I struggle during these days, and with those around me I'm helping, I must show postiveness as I feel negative thoughts and feelings of self-pity. You have socialized me, Doug. When I was in the world living on the streets, riding the rails, I never felt this damn lonely. I actually sat under my table last night wrapped up and bawled my eyes out.

A Slap in the Face

Tad

I'm loyal to the wrong people. I let some guys in the barracks use me. The whole time I was thinking that I was doing the right thing and helping them but they were lying to me. In the end it cost me $50. I don't care about the money, really. It was the fact I put myself out there and got used. Roy and I talked about it and he said I need to quit trying to help people that have no intention of helping themselves.

Roy slapped me in the face [with his words]. At first I took his words as cruel. Here is how it went down. I was in the shower that is directly in front of Roy's cell, about 60 feet out. We were talking about me trying to change the people, police as well, because what happened the day before with these guys using me and the police lying all the time. I was telling Roy I feel that if I don't try to make a change, then I feel I let myself down. He said I needed to take off my Superman cape and quit trying to save everyone. Then I said, "f– it. I'll just give up then." He told me, "Kill yourself then. I got a razor if you need it." I didn't say anything else but got out of the shower and put my head down and tucked my tail between my legs.

I went to my cell and lay down on my rack, thinking about what had just happened, asking myself, "Why would Roy say that?" Then I thought about the past and I realized that over the years I've gotten myself into trouble trying to help people who in the end never said thanks or showed appreciation because they were so wrapped up in themselves. They didn't care. Then it hit me. Roy was teaching me something and the only way to get my attention was to say those cruel words. Now all I can do is bow to him three times when I can. He has helped me see compassion from a different side: "Quit putting yourself out there to be used, whether with police or inmates."

The next day I got an email from you with "Activity in the Heart of Samantabhadra" [a Buddhist scripture that describes bringing to fruition the seed of Great Love found within us all]. After I read it, tears started to fall. It is amazing how the "pull" is so great with us. What made you decide to pick this teaching and send it to me? All of this has shown me how blinding the discriminating mind can be. I've found the meditation hall within me.

You wrote to me recently: "Hope you are able to practice in the face of all the discouraging news." Now I see clearly, even in my moments of "nothing" that practice is still going on. Bad days or good days, it's still practice. Yes, I was "lost" but the dharma showed me I'm right where I need to be in my present moment.

Even as he continued his practice, Tad struggled with feelings of anger in the wake of what he saw as his uncle's manipulation of his grandmother, and her subsequent death.

My grandmother was the one who was going to assist me with funds to help pay for my counseling, parole fees, fines, clothing cost, etc., until I got on my feet. I am hurt and pissed, so I talked to an officer about putting me on "single man statues" (being by myself) so I can think and not lose my cool or do anything to harm anyone else. They said they can't help me because it's not an emergency. Here I am with a serious issue, asking for help and these officers tell me they can't help me. So what did I do? I caught disciplinary just so I can be locked down by myself. I wrote a grievance telling them "The next inmate they try to force in my cell I am going to stab." The Captain came and talked to me, telling me "You know I can write you up for this." I said, "I don't care. You would rather see me hurt another inmate than help me. Lock me up." So finally they put me by myself. Playing their game was the only way they would put me by myself. Sad. What the public doesn't know is a man was just killed here last week because of being forced to be with someone in his cell. He kept telling the officers they were violating his rights and to get the other guy out of his cell. Well, they didn't, so he cut his throat.

I asked Tad if he felt his mindfulness practice would help him better handle his anger in the future.

Would I be more in control now if the same situation happened (pertaining to my grandma)? No, I would still handle the situation the same in prison: I would separate myself. Would my practice prepare me to deal with a similar situation in the future? Yes. That's the reason to separate myself. Discipline myself to not be selfish. If out of anger I hurt someone else just because I think it would make me hurt less, that action would be out of pure selfish ignorance. I would be no better than the act my uncle pulled to create the situation. Once we see the bigger picture we can question the moral situation and can see how not to live by the actions of others who live in vain. We can focus upon the bigger picture. I felt I handled the situation very well compared to how I would have years ago.

. . . .

Compassion must come before kindness. When dealing with [prison] officers, if an officer (just as an inmate) takes your kindness for weakness, it only makes the officer worse in their own selfish ego. There are times, out of compassion, to truly help in guiding an officer or inmate, you must be aggressive. This aggression will force them to rethink their direction in life. In this environment, just as in society, you must pay attention to people's characters. Some pretend to be mean-hearted, when others are just plain evil. Compassion is about being mindful of what is needed for the betterment of an individual or individuals. Right and wrong in many people's eyes, goes out the window! Did Roy forget already the day he "Slapped me in the face?" Out of compassion, he had to do it! To get me to see my erroneous ways. It doesn't matter if a person is in a white ADC suit or a blue correctional suit ... it is the person within!

Compassion, in truth, is "wise discernment" and kindness is a by-product. True selfless kindness, that is!!

On that same page you asked for reactions/comments to Bruno's statement, "Is there heaven just outside of the hell we're living in?" I personally do not believe in hell! I believe it is made up to scare people. Why do I believe this? Because once I saw life in a universal perspective, there is no need for a hell. If one truly understands our duty in this life, there is no right or wrong. There is only the purpose. How we are programmed to express our motives and intentions shows our level of understanding of "selfless universal compassion."

A better example ... there is a guy that lives downstairs. He talks about child molesters all the time. How all they do is destroy kids' lives. (And I don't deny this.) But ... the deep root truth is a child's life is being destroyed. This same guy will later get on the tier and talk about "How much he loves his kids," who are very young. I asked him one day, "How can you talk about another man (child molester) destroying a child's life, when you yourself are destroying your own kids' lives?" Yep. He got mad at that, but it was true. I pointed out to him. You're 26 years old. You've been to prison three times.

You were out 44 days this last time. "Do your kids mean that little to you … that dope (meth) is more important? You are purposely destroying your own kids' lives by not being there as the father, which is your Duty to be." When one finally sees this universal duty to compassion, you no longer get a choice. It is a duty. Why is it a duty? Karma!! And in my perspective, my heaven is my karma! Turning my bad karma into grace is the heaven part. Karma is the feedback, universal feedback—that is!

During his time in prison, Tad reflected on his relationship with his mother, and eventually reconnected with her.

Her boss bought her a cell phone just so she and I could talk (great guy) She told me "thank you." I'm the only child of hers that talks to her on this level. She is now back in church and back on a positive spiritual path. And guess what? Her pastor is a serious art lover. So yes, I've been donating artwork to be auctioned off at his church! 25% goes to the church and 75% goes to a local children's organization.

· · · · · · · ·

My mom wrote me a three-page letter telling me how thankful she was. I don't think she ever wrote me a three-page letter before. She said, "It's funny. You're in prison and keep your word and these people I have to deal with on a daily basis couldn't tell the truth or stand on their word to save their lives." That made me feel good! And that moment would not have been possible without you.

Tad told me about how a guard's lie got him into trouble. I wrote back asking him to explain what had happened.

I truly believe I willed a certain chain of events into play without realizing it was for the spiritual teachings of the dharma the whole time. These "willed events" I believe started in another life, such as coming to prison, reuniting with Lisa, meeting Roy, Miss Linda, and you. I mean, I can keep going, but an officer lies about me [writing him up for an improper action with a female guard] and yes, at the moment, all I could think about going home was being destroyed [because of the infraction with the officer, Tad's parole was postponed]. Here is where it gets interesting … how everything has played out so far:

1. I get a disciplinary due to more lies [by the female guard], like the ones that put me in prison [for the alleged rape], which makes my emotions run wild.

2. Mindfulness practice comes in and I focus upon what's important in the moment and controlling my emotions.

3. I get a letter from Roy and after reading it a few times, I realize the emotions connected with the lies are gone. And all I can feel now is compassion for Roy. Then I start thinking about your medical condition and I realize my moment is nothing compared to the two of yours.

4. I get three letters from you. One with the forms [required to submit my art to an exhibition], one with the pictures of your family moments, and [one with] the quote from the Surangama [a Buddhist scripture]. And the merit Miss Linda and you sent for the encounter with the officer and for strength for mindfulness and kindness through Roy's moments with the guards included.

5. I get [a draft of this book] back just as they are locking me up in the Hole.

All this came at the perfect moment. If I hadn't been lied about, the book would have been sent back already [because I would have been released on parole]. The merit and encouragement from Miss Linda, Roy, and you would never have been. If I had not been in a one-man cell I would not have had the meditation time to sit and think about all this and would not have realized it was for the dharma. Embedded deep within this emotional roller-coaster of a single moment, was another step in spiritual understanding. And that lasts forever, not just for the moment.

In the Surangama text you sent me it states that "first I redirected my hearing inward in order to enter the current of the sages." This is what brought all this realization full circle. The most important element in this is my karma. Without my positive karma, this wouldn't have had time to accrue. Without assistance of proper guidance (from you, Roy, materials sent, etc.) of mindfulness, compassion, kindness, etc., this positive karma would not have come to be. Without the karma, the chain of events that led to this very moment of understanding would never have been possible.

And yes, getting the book back and being able to read it a couple more times really helped my moment of need. It helped me see a lot more about the inner beauty of the dharma. John, Cody, and Roy talk about moments of need for the teachings in their situations. That is their need. This is my need, for the truth of the teachings serves everyone differently, just as they need it for their spiritual journeys.

· · · · · · · ·

Yes, as we practice letting go, compassion, meditation, we see the field of flowers in a wider view. We lose ourselves in the field of flowers. At times it is hard to believe I could be used to bring love, kindness, ethical help into peoples' lives.

As the only member of our group who would ever leave prison, Tad chose to formally become a Buddhist after his release, so he could complete the Jukai ceremony as a free man.

CHAPTER 17

A DANGEROUS PLACE

Having already been imprisoned for nine years and facing the rest of his life behind bars, Cody often looked to his friendship with Roy and me as his only solace. Then Cody called to tell me he was being moved to another prison. He was no longer in the Hole, in fact, he was working outside when a guard came and told him he was being transferred. He was unable to say goodbye to Roy, knowing they would likely never see each other again. And the sad fact is, prisoners can't write to each other.

Cody

[The guards] really do treat him [a new neighbor, an inmate with cognitive disabilities] bad and make fun of him sometimes and don't even feed him. So I made a fishing line the other day and when he didn't get anything to eat, I had to smash a sandwich so it would fit through the door. He took it and didn't say nothing back. He still hasn't said anything. When I go to the store I'm going to buy a bag of hard candy and throw the fella some. I always think about what Roy would do. I really miss my Buddy Roy, Bro. He taught me some good shit and I finally got my ass in gear and started to walk the path and spread the kindness.

Cody decided to clean the bathroom and shower area as an act of kindness to the other prisoners and an opportunity for him to practice mindful kindness.

I'm still taking small steps to understand. I was proud of how mindful I was about the task ahead and took my time to clean the big shower. It really surprised me how many people came to me and said, "Hey Cody, I appreciate you cleaning the shower, man." It was a really good feeling because I know they don't like to shower in a nasty shower. So from now on I'm going to get up every morning and start my day by cleaning the shower so at the end of the day everyone will see the kindness and might learn from my little hour of compassion.

. . . .

Most barracks in prison have 50 or 60 people in one living quarter. There are racks, which are beds side by side. The bathroom has about five toilets and seven sinks you are responsible for. There are barrack's porters twice a day and two at night and a kind thing to do for them is to put your shoes at the end of your rack so that it's much easier for them to sweep and mop around the rack. Some will say thank you. Now a typical prisoner is not a kind person in this situation and might start a fight or curse at the porter when he is just doing his job. If you were mindful, then you would realize the kindness of just putting your shoes and laundry bags at the end of the rack.

. . . .

Every Monday they bring us one roll of toilet paper to last a whole week. I never thought I would have to be mindful of how much paper to use until last week when I ran out on Friday. This was the cause of my suffering. I was really nice to an officer and gave him some hard candy and asked if he would please get me some toilet paper and when he went on break and came back with a [package of four rolls], I broke the roll down four ways and gave him three back and asked him to please give the three to other people who were asking for some. I have really come a long way Bro. I could have taken the whole four rolls for myself. It feels good not to be like that anymore.

———————————————

Gradually, I began to trusty Cody again. As the weeks went by and he wrote me about his mindfully kind cleaning and the kindness he was showing to other prisoners, I felt he was beginning to truly understand the principles we were practicing. Still, while I occasionally sent him small amounts of money for special occasions like his birthday, or to buy his daughter Christmas presents, I never resumed sending him a monthly allowance for kind acts, as I did with Roy and John.

While at the Cummins Unit, Cody continued to receive medical care for his brain tumor and was sent to the University of Arkansas Medical Center for surgery—a rare trip outside the prison walls. It was also a rare opportunity to see his family. His girlfriend and daughter, still a baby, were allowed to visit him in the hospital. For the first and probably only time in his life, Cody was able to hold his daughter. Cody survived the surgery, but developed vision and mobility problems on his right side, for which he received physical therapy.

I went to the hospital for testing. It took a young woman a long time to hook up the [electrodes] to my head. She doesn't get frustrated with all the wires. She told me she has to be calm and knows what she is doing is helping the doctor and the patient. I said, "So you are just being mindful." She said, "Yes," and that it makes her feel good that she is helping someone with their suffering. Wow.

········

As time went on I got to order my own food [at the hospital] and I went to the TV room and I met an older woman there. You could tell she had been there for a long time and she worked the afternoon night shift. But she would get me ice cream and spend all night long without looking at me like some of the others nurses who judge me because I have shackles on my feet. But it was cool to see and experience kindness.

········

I was riding in the car [going back to the prison] and it was just me and I had a chain on my feet and handcuffs. There was a cage between me and the two officers. I treated them with respect and guess what? After we left Little Rock, they stopped to get something to eat at Sonic and I said, "Can I please get a burger and fries?" and I told them I got life without and the chances of me ever eating at Sonic again is slim, and one woman officer got me a #2. I was thankful for her kindness as I ate the burger and I took calm breaths and ate it slowly to enjoy every flavor.

········

Every human being in here has his own way of doing time. Some guys in here get caught up in the system games and go with the flow. I know this because I'm still working on my own self too and sometimes fall into system games and get off my path, and the reason is I'm not using my energy for ways of kindness. But when I'm mindful and on my kindness path, time is so much easier and nicer. I even get so that sometimes I forget I'm in prison.

. . . .

What I've been noticing here in prison is everybody is in their own category. The Mexicans have the MS13 [gang] and are family. The Blacks are in all kinds of gangs and the whites are in a few different Aryan Brotherhoods. But I sit and listen to all of the different beings and notice how much they really take care of each other with kindness. If you are involved with them you're going to be taken care of. I heard a guy holler out to a Buddy in Aryan Brotherhood and say "Hey, Bro, I'm going to the store next week, you need anything? I'm going to get you a bag of coffee and a few soups." I hear that and smile. It's really cool to see the kindness and compassion that all these different beings have. They may be in these gangs and have their beliefs, but they are all still good people and got kindness in their heart.

. . . .

The guy next to me that is going home in two months is New Aryan Empire and told me the other day that he would want to propose me in. I told him I'm good. He said, "Well, you're a good dude Cody and you're white. You can be a part of the Brotherhood."

This is what happened. It was Friday night and some gang members were playing dice and came up to me and said, "Hey White Boy, climb up the bars and put grease on the camera so they can't see us playing dice." I said, "No bro', I ain't f–ing with the cameras." Then eight members of the G.D. Gang and B.D. Gang surrounded me in the corner and said they was going to beat my ass if I didn't do it. Well I told them that is what is going to have to happen and I was jumped by eight members. After they were done they told me if I did not put grease on the camera they were going to stab me, so I walked in front of the camera, hoping that the guards would see me doing this. Well, they did not see me until after I told them. Anyway, I was told not to go to chow, but as soon as the door opened I ran to the Sgt. and they put me in handcuffs and took me to the infirmary. Then I was sent out to the hospital. I came back and now they locked me up back in super max on what we call P.C. or Protective Custody and today I finally got my stuff back or what stuff that was not stolen. I've sent you the Master Disciplinary Form so you would not think I'm crying to you.

I tried to explain that I tried to cover the camera with grease because my life was threatened, but they asked me why I didn't tell the guard on the door and I explained that I would have been stabbed. But this prison is so f–ed up. They told me when they brought me all my stuff today that I would have to fill out a stolen property form and they would try to get my stuff back. I'm just thankful I'm alive, really blessed that I did not get too badly hurt. The ribs and the black eyes will heal. I'm going to be in this cell now for a long time. If I tried to get out then other members of the gangs would probably do something bad to me for telling the police how they all jumped on me, but I have learned to like this cell by myself. I've got a shower in my cell and a TV, and I don't have to worry about my life when I do sleep. No one can steal that from me.

Cody was soon taken out of protective custody and sent to the Hole for 30 days, as punishment for defacing the security cameras.

I have started Day One [in the Hole] so far it has been good. I have a lot more time to get my head clear and not wander around. I have me a Cell Buddy; it's a cricket and she or he will sing all night long and I love it. For my first night of meditation I put two hours in and I started over about seven times, then when I got still and my body calm and my mind clear I was seeing footsteps on sand. After that I did my yoga and sleep was really good.

After 30 days in the Hole, Cody was moved to a different cell block.

All I can see out my new cell block window is the next cell block wall. No grass, just cars and a little of the sky and I've got the loudest neighbor ever. I think this is a test for me on all the meditation I've been doing for the past two months. This past week has been a real challenge on sitting, but I realized: Let it go, count my breaths, and feel the air going in and out through my nose hairs. It did not take long and I was there. But the guy next to me is really disrespectful. He is in the gang that jumped on me. At that time, one of his homeboys kicked me in the face so he talks shit about it all the time and tries to drive me about it, so for the past week I've been listening to my radio a lot.

········

I've been through a tough time with the guy next to me. It's not that easy to let go, but I'm learning how. I'm turning this into positive. As I was meditating I busted out in tears and I used the moment to feel the tears roll down my face—tears of pain, my past wrongs, my downfalls, my hunger, my joy, my kindness, my happiness. Those were the thoughts with each tear I wiped off my face and smiled because not a damn thing matters but how I handle the moment ahead. It is hard with the guy next to me who is so loud, so I take my radio and put it on AM to static and I can do my five sittings a day. This guy made my last weeks crazy; he has told everyone around me I'm gay and that I have done this and that and I just laugh. I don't understand why he has so much hate. I guess making stuff up about me is how he tries to hide his pain, but he does not understand that he will suffer until he takes control over his mind.

· · · · · · · ·

It's been a long week. They came to my cell and told me to pack up because they are moving me to population [from segregation]. I said I wouldn't go because the gang that jumped me knows. I told the officers about it and that they will probably do it again. So they took me to the Hole and wrote me up, so now I'm in the Hole for three weeks but at least I'm not next to the guy that was really stressing me out. I have nothing as of right now, but I think this is good because I'm going to take my time and do some deep meditation.

As he came to terms with life in prison, Cody also tried to maintain his ties with his family, including his daughter, Blossom; her mother, Autumn; and her grandmother, Alma. Cody considers Maryjo, his daughter's half-sister, as part of his family as well.

I got a letter back from Alma, Autumn's Grandma. She told me about how bad the year had been for her and that she lost her sister, her best friend, and that she was depressed. So I wrote her a letter back and said that her kindness and compassion for me shows what kind of person she is and that stuff happens in life all the time that we don't understand, but if we show kindness to others and surround ourselves with positive things, it will make our day a lot better. She wrote me back saying I made her feel better and that Blossom does make her day a lot better. She is really a sweet woman.

· · · · · · · ·

Cody phoned to give me the news from his sister. Autumn's mother had turned Autumn in to the Department of Human Services for child neglect. The state took custody of Cody's daughter, Blossom, and Autumn's one-month-old baby, Maryjo. Cody feels Blossom and Maryjo will be better off in foster care.

I had to ask you about sending a book or toy to Blossom and Maryjo for Xmas. They like Dora the Explorer and Mrs. Kitty. I'm sure Mrs. Linda could find the girls something good. She liked the Bear last year. If you could put "To Blossom from Daddy Cody Shane Griffin" and on the other "To Maryjo from Daddy Cody Shane Griffin." My little girl is growing up fast. I can't wait until she is old enough to talk to you and hear your wonderful teachings.

. . . .

I just got off the phone with you. When you told me that you got the stuff for Blossom and Maryjo for Xmas, tears of joy filled my eyes. Thank you a lot. It means more than you can imagine.

. . . .

I got the newspaper the other day and saw that my brother was in jail, so I wrote him a long letter telling him how bad this place really is. So I hope he takes it all to heart and gets back on track. I guess he and my sister ain't that close to me because growing up we were all separated. To be honest, we really only spent seven years of our lives around each other and I have done my sister wrong in the past when I was bad on meth.

. . . .

My sister really did take me in and gave me a place to stay when she did not have to and all I would care about was running around with friends and hanging out with people who really did not care. When I look back now I see that all I was doing was using my sister for a place to come to sleep, eat, shower, and have sex with girls. Then I was out the door to chase fun and when my sister's boyfriend who was an auto mechanic worked his ass off fixing cars and got deported due to not having papers, I starting stealing tools out of his shop.

. . . .

My sister caught me one day when I was smoking meth with and having sex with two girls. She kicked me out and told my niece and nephew I was a bad person. I stayed with a friend until I ended up on the streets. I slept in a church van outside a church at night and a car that was in the parking lot of the skating rink. I was thinking about all the bad things I have done that caused this bad karma and that is what makes me want to do so many kind things. It really makes me open my eyes and say, "Damn, I got so much to learn and so much good to do with the rest of my life."

Shakedown

I call the practice I've been doing for the past two weeks my Inter-cell-walls of Happiness. I take a newspaper and open it up and use it like a poster board. I have pictures on it I took out of magazines that are all positive. I have four poster boards made like this and which take up one whole side of my wall. The first week of trying this out I kept having problems with officers telling me every morning to take the damn stuff off my wall; those are the rules. So my mindfulness went to work and I had to change a few things. I came up with My Floor Full of Happiness. I leave a path to my toilet and my door and I use the newspaper because it can all be picked up and folded and put away as needed. This practice of surrounding myself with positive things, including animal pictures, has helped me. It's a really cool thing and I'm digging it.

· · · · · · · ·

I got a wakeup call at 4:30 a.m. for a shakedown. I really ain't a happy camper in the morning and I had six officers in my cell telling me to get up, take off my clothes, put my hands behind my back, walk to my cell door backwards, and get down on my knees with my hands on my head. Butt naked. Not only is this just humiliating, but if you don't do it fast enough they will pepper-spray you. Bro, I came close but did what they wanted with a smile as they threw everything around and made as big a mess as they could. I asked the officer if he would be careful with the newspaper I had folded up and he just opened it and shook it all over my cell and I didn't have any anger.

· · · · · · · ·

It was so easy to let it go the whole time and I was thinking, well, I can clean my cell a lot better and I have been meaning to throw that away, and redo my Wall of Happiness. When they left I said, "Thank you, I will see you all again next time. Have a good day." I'm so at peace with myself and much kinder, no stress. I thank a lot of people in here. Bro, I realize that when I get off into meditation, I'm not even here. I'm in the forest like the picture you sent me of you and Mrs. Linda. I know living in a cell like this ain't good, but when I'm in this cell I focus more on kindness, mindfulness. I can meditate in peace. I keep healthy and my mind sharp. A lot of people go crazy, but I seem to find myself well.

. . . .

In my next letter to Cody, I asked him to look deeper at himself and reflect on why he responded to the shakedown as he did: "Think about whether you irritated them by wishing them a nice day and if having them be irritated is what you want."

I really did not have any anger at all so I did practice what you were talking about with the Shakedown and yeah, I can see now where I should have used kindness more in a positive way. Wow, thanks for that teaching. I will put it to work, Bro.

. . . .

But you know what? This is where the problem had festered within my mind. Instead of looking at the outside, I began looking at the inside and started dwelling on my surroundings and self. I lost track of my goal and intent in life—to help others.

. . . .

This weekend we had an officer they call Tank working on the block. He does what he can to wake us up just to get us to react. He uses what's called a Bean Flip to open the hinges of the door and he uses it in a way that makes all types of noise. I could hear him coming so I got up while I was brushing my teeth and was listening to everybody else using their energy to cuss him, calling him everything under the sun and I thought, that is why they mess with the crazy ones. So when he got to my door I had a smile on my face and kind words because I could have awakened with anger and talked shit, but I realize that would have taken happiness out of my day.

. . . .

The other day I went to sit and I was one with the sound of the raindrops. It was really cool. Now I have been getting in my window when the sun is shining and feel it on my face. I get out of this place all the way until I open my eyes. I never knew that meditation could be this cool. I have been moved to a new cell block and have new people all around so I'm still listening to people talk to see how I can talk too and understand.

. . . .

I was in the Hole and could only get outside for a half hour on some days. Outside was an 8' by 8' concrete floor with high walls. I badly wanted to see grass. Because of the high walls I could not see grass but they had just mowed it and I could smell the grass. In my meditation I pictured you mowing the grass to help my practice. Through your eyes I was able to see the grass.

. . . .

The last two days there have been ants in my cell but I don't kill them. I watch them and now I realize that when I was outside and got into an ant bed and they bit me those ants were different than these ants, which are getting away from the cold outside. If I drop food, they get a little crazy so I put bread in the corner of my cell every day and let them enjoy it and it keeps them over in the corner and not all around my cell. Those ants have a life just like me and I leave them alone and they leave me alone. There aren't that many of them—about 12—so it ain't bad. They stay in their corner and I hope this don't sound crazy because I was just sharing some crazy kindness to a small family of ants.

. . . .

I was talking with a guy that seemed to enjoy what I was sharing with him on the Dharma and the vent was opened so we could communicate. A few guys were listening as I talked about some crickets that I didn't want killed just because they were making noise in a guy's cell. I asked him to just throw the crickets out of his cell. Well, when I went out into the yard call the other day, there was a Mexican guy and he said, "Hey Cody, check this out," and he had about six crickets in his pocket that he then let go outside. I said thank you, and he smiled. Pretty cool.

On January 21, 2015, Cody formally became a Buddhist by going through a shortened version of the Jukai ceremony.

Well, Bro, it is official. I just got back in my cell from the ceremony. Woah, Rev. Leon was amazing. It was behind the glass but I still understood and knew what I was there for. I think it went really well. I had a feeling of relief and ease. He answered a lot of my questions and just seeing a monk, the real deal, and just taking my Precepts that I will live by. I went into the visitation with a clear, open mind. I brought just me myself, Bro. I have thrown away past evil and have been converted to the truth.

Rev. Leon Kackman

Things went well yesterday with Cody—he seemed bright and together and said that it was one of the best days of his life. We visited for a while and then did the ceremony across the glass in a non-contact visit. Somehow this visit had its own particular sadness for me since he is so young (he was born the year after I first took the precepts). I have been reflecting over the last little while that samsara [life cycle] really has its own kind of teeth and is a dangerous place.

CHAPTER 18

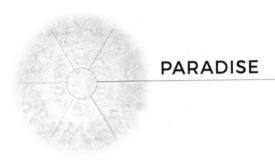

PARADISE

My wife, Linda, felt strongly that we should visit Roy in prison, and I agreed.

We arrived at the Tucker Unit of the Arkansas Department of Corrections on the afternoon of June 25th, 2013. It was 90 degrees, with humidity of 95 percent. Looking past the end of the parking lot, we watched as inmates, dressed in white, walked single file, returning to the prison from working on the prison farm. Following each group of a dozen prisoners was a guard dressed in black, on horseback.

As we approached the box-like security building, I could hear all sorts of birds singing, but I couldn't see them. Some may have been roosting underneath the guard tower, or possibly in the well-trimmed shrubs in front of these buildings. The fence looked just like what you see in prison movies or on the news—high, probably 12-foot chain link, two rows of heavy razor wire curling along the top edge, and electrical units mounted on each of the heavy metal posts.

All the workers in the Security building were African-American. The woman at the desk smiled at us and said she recognized our names from the many letters I had sent. The guard in charge of admittance, a Ms. Edwards, wasn't so friendly, but was very professional, making it clear we were not allowed to bring in any pictures, lipstick, pens, pencils, notepaper, any of Roy's letters, our Buddhist scripture book, or Linda's knitting. She also told Linda she could not wear her shawl, because the prisoners could see her shoulders, and told us to drive to town and buy a jacket. Luckily I had an extra long-sleeved shirt in the car, and after Linda put it on, she was allowed to enter. The guard then electronically verified our driver's licenses, photographed us, and took the fingerprints of our left index fingers.

After passing through three locked gates, we reached the waiting room. After about 15 minutes, Roy entered—weak and using a cane, and yet, incongruously, escorted by two stern guards. We studied him as he settled in to the visitation cubicle, seeing him for the first time after almost four years of letter writing. He was so weak, he could barely stand, but gave us a beaming smile. We immediately reached our hands up to the thick glass.

Through the glass, he placed his hands against each of ours. Tears filled his and Linda's eyes. For several long minutes, we had a hard time even looking at one another, but just stood together in silence.

We were in the no-contact visitation room, with eight cubicles on each side, painted an institutional pale green. We were the only ones in the room. The three-inch high screen below the window looked as if it had been painted to close up the holes that allow sound to pass through. It's hard to hear, and sometimes we had to bend down closer to the screen to hear what Roy was saying. It seemed every time we tried chanting a scripture for Roy, there was either a crowd of guards talking and laughing around the corner from the visitation area or someone was making a huge racket filling the rows of vending machines that stood just outside the door in the hall.

Roy's personal guard, Ms. J. was responsible for listening in on our conversation to make sure we did not discuss forbidden topics like escape or smuggling in contraband. She sat on the countertop of the row of windows behind us the whole time we were with Roy. He smiled warmly as he introduced her and told us what a good soul she was, and her partner as well. She didn't seem friendly; she seemed exhausted. At one point we looked back and she was sleeping with her head perched on the top of her bulletproof vest. Roy commented that it made a good headrest. (John later wrote that "Lady J" presents an air of boredom but is known for her live-and-let-live attitude toward the prisoners—while also commanding respect. "Don't mistake her because she's fat," he said. "She benches 300 pounds, is a lesbian with a wife of 16 years, and is very cool. I see inmates try to grab her and I've seen her take each one and literally put them in unbreakable holds or slam them to the ground, laughing while she does it.")

Roy had an engaging smile and expressive face, with a palpable warmth and light in his dark brown eyes. He looked to be around five feet, seven inches in height, and thin, maybe 140 lbs. His salt and pepper hair was thinning at the crown, and his cheeks were sunken due to tooth loss.

Expressing embarrassment that he did not have his top teeth in, Roy's upper lip curled over his gums. Both his arms were almost solid sleeves of tattoos, which included the wheel of life on one forearm, as well as six primary symbols from Tibetan Buddhism, and the Chinese characters for Buddha on the inside of his left wrist. The back of his left arm was adorned with a picture of the Buddha in meditation with a baby Buddha sitting on his lap, both sitting on a lotus flower. Just above his right wrist were the words, "noble silence." He showed us part of the scar from his back surgery.

Roy told us that he had been looking forward to our visit and was so excited that he had not been able to sleep the night before we arrived. We chatted for a few minutes about the size of the prison and about his special handicap-accessible cell, which has two four-inch mattresses instead of one because of his back problems. He answered Linda's question about the location of "the Hole." He replied that there are actually 30 "Holes," all with an extra door for added security and no air-conditioning. He then showed us the slight swelling of his hands and a couple of small scars on his face from abuse by his father when he was 10.

We meditated for 20 minutes, in silence, in this formal, uninviting, no-contact room. Roy then shared some of the teachings he had recently read, for example, that smiles require no maintenance, do not cost anything to give, and at the end of the day the supply is still endless. Another was WOW, "Wishing Others Well," especially when anger arises toward those you are with. Roy told us that the guard who had escorted him to the visiting room was often angry and mean—he believes she is bipolar. He said her daughter, also a guard, is delightful. Roy had recently had a challenging encounter with this guard and said he responded to her angry attacks with smiles and wishes for well-being. By the end of the exchange, she thanked him.

Roy paused, and brushed away a fly. "I don't kill them, so my cell is full of flies," he said.

A concerned sergeant stopped by and asked us to encourage Roy to eat more so he would stop losing weight. Roy replied that he had not eaten meat for about a year. I explained to him that many Buddhists eat meat and even Buddhist leaders in vegetarian traditions eat meat if their health problems require meat in their diet. Roy said that the meat and other foods are usually terrible. I reminded him of a description of Burmese monks I had sent him; they ate whatever they were given, including meat. They were not allowed to cook because they would be inclined to cook food that they liked, strengthening their attachments to certain tastes. With Roy's deteriorating skeletal system, maintaining muscle tone is critical, which requires protein. In a prison setting, that means eating meat.

He showed us the exercises he was doing to regain the use of his hands and delay the loss of his ability to walk. These were also the exercises that helped bring him out of his depression.

We talked about the need for Buddhist materials written at a simple level for two prisoners who had low reading comprehension. Roy regretted not realizing sooner that a prisoner to whom he had sent maybe 20 Buddhist books was not able to read or understand them. We read a "kite," held up to the thick glass, that the prisoner had sent Roy about wanting so badly to know what was in the books—heartbreaking.

In the two hours allowed for our visit, we discussed a wide range of topics. Roy had recommended that all the partners read Thich Nhat Hanh's *The Heart of Buddha's Teaching,* an excellent foundation. I asked him about the book *The Shack,* by William P. Young, which a minister told me was very helpful in teaching prisoners about the Christian faith. Roy says the book was really not about Christianity per se. He felt the book gave the reader a rationale for being positive.

In a recent letter Roy had asked if hope, defined as expecting or wanting something, suggests that the present moment is lacking and that instead the person should look toward the future. I told Roy I agreed that looking to the future can undermine mindfulness practice in the present moment.

As our visit drew to a close, well after the two-hour maximum had expired, Roy was not able to find a comfortable way to stand, so he quickly agreed to the suggestion to sit, which allowed him to handle his pain. After a short meditation, we again joined palms against the glass and bowed to each other. The uncertainty of Roy's health made our farewell painful. Tearfully, Linda told him she was honored to be able to meet such a wonderful teacher of the dharma.

To leave, we had to again have our driver's licenses electronically verified, our picture taken, and the fingerprint of our left index finger taken. We walked the cement path to the outer security building and then out its door. While we had initially been viewed with suspicion—why would two well educated, reasonably well-off individuals travel 2,000 miles to visit Roy Tester, whom we had never before met?—the prison staff seemed to have grown more accepting.

Thoroughly intimidated by the atmosphere of the prison, we cautiously drove out of the area, keeping well below the speed limit. We weren't going to take any chances of getting into trouble.

We returned to Eugene and resumed our regular lives. Sometimes, driving around on my errands, I think of Roy in that hard, impersonal room. And I think of his letters, where he writes the return address, "PARADISE," and I cry.

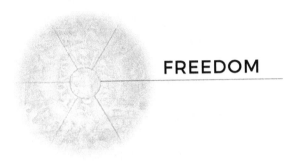

CHAPTER 19

FREEDOM

Cody

I'm writing to let you know I'm not really proud of something I did and I hope you are not mad at me. I don't know what I was thinking but this is what happened. We have plenty of glass in our cells that covers our light. Well, a guy told me how to cut a hole [that served as a way of passing notes to the cell above] and I did and got caught. I did get wrote up and 30 days in the Hole, [demoted to] Class 4, and I got to pay $381.89 [for the damage].

I really need help now. I let you down Doug. I don't want to do this "life without" no more. It is the same shit every day. I really just want to tie a sheet up and hang myself over this stupid shit I did. I know you and Mrs. Linda is going to be mad at me. Ya'll is all I got and I do so good for a while and one little f–in' thing I f– up and just want to end this. I will understand if you never want to write to me no more.

· · · · · · · ·

Well Partner, it took me a while to think really hard. I slipped up, stumbled, and made a mistake in my journey. As I set in this Hole and look deep, I realize hey, this is going to happen. This is just another teaching and lesson well learned in my path. Yes, I really wanted to end everything but I thought, how can I end something that never really began? Now is what we have in our journey. Suffering is going to happen. Letting go, learning from this bump and moving forward. Yesterday was yesterday. Tomorrow is tomorrow. Now this moment I'm in, now is all that matters. This has really helped me. I realize I have a problem with worrying about what happened in the past and looking forward to the future. Now I'm sitting and focusing on this moment. My chest rises in with a cool breath, out with lowering chest. Monkey mind, where did you go now? Air out my nose, movement of my toes as I sit still in this hole.

. . . .

I just got done meditating. I was really having a hard time. Let me explain. I got a card from Alma, Autumn's Grandma. This is what she said word for word: "Cody, I can't help what Autumn does or don't do. She don't write anyone. Candy [Autumn's aunt] will not let [the girls] go to a prison. Candy says it will scar them all their life. I'm sure she will let them come if they want to when they turn 18. I have worked all day and can't think. We will send you pictures of them when we got them. Chin up, you'll see your darling girl someday. Love, Alma"

Now Doug, I just got done sitting and when I came out at the end of the 20 minutes, Blossom came in my mind as I was trying to let it go and come back to my breathing. I had tears rolling down my face. I kept my posture and remained sitting, letting tears roll out. That letter really hit me, Bro, and I know I need to let it go, Bro, but that is my girl that is my blood that is all I got left. I want her to go to college and live the life I did not get to. She is in a really good place with Autumn's Aunt Candy, so that was coming in my mind. I took a deep breath and smiled at it and made my path my way. Only I can control how my outcome will be. I have to realize that everything is a teaching. That is what all of us have to realize and approach things because in a crazy way the letter or card from Alma makes me dry my eyes, write you now, and take a deep breath and bow to you, Doug, and thank you for the teachings that you have given me. My choice is to let it go, to live for this path and continue to show compassion to everyone and everything.

. . . .

I was sent to VSM Examination Room on 5-30-15 to see Dr. Bland for chronic care. When I was seated on an exam bed she was sitting behind a desk with a computer and stated to me that I was seeing her for my chronic care on my Hep-C. She stated that my last lab was good and that my levels were good. She asked me why I was taking Gabapentin AKA Narotin 800 mg three times a day. I told her I had been taking this medication for over a year and it was for the nerve damage in my left lower leg and foot and my index finger in between the bone where I had to have surgery to put the tendon back together, which didn't go well and now I cannot bend my finger. The nerve pain gives me problems all the time. Also my back hurts, which was injured last year by falling. The nerve hurts and little movements hurt.

I told her that the drug helps me a lot and I'm able to get up and move around a lot better. I asked her why she would discontinue a medication that is working for me and that I've been on for two years. She said then that it's because it has benefits. I asked what she meant and she said "getting high." Now this is a non-narcotic [drug] and I told her that. She said, "Well, your back x-rays is good," and I said that it does not show my nerves, only the bone, and I said I needed a proper MRI of my back and she told the officers she was done with me and to get me out and back to my cell. I had told her my weight is 209 pounds and that I'm starting a hunger strike until my medication is back and that I could not deal with the pain of getting out of bed to eat or use the restroom because it hurts too much without the medication. She then stated, "So?"

Now I'm having to fill out this affidavit stating how it's not right to take me off the medication I've been taking for over two years. I feel you've got to stand up for what is right because if you don't stand up for something you will fall for anything and I'm sticking with this hunger strike not only for me, but Roy and all beings having to suffer for the lack of proper medical treatment.

. . . .

I just got back from the doctor. I went to sick call at 11:37 a.m. The nurse asked how long I had been on the hunger strike and I told her five days. She took my weight and I was 202 pounds. I was 210 when I started and she said that I had lost a lot of weight and that I would need to be seen right now. This was good, and I actually got a burst of energy from the joy of getting to see the Dr. that had me on Narotin in the first place. I told her I was on a hunger strike because my meds were discontinued and I was not even looked at or examined.

I asked her to please be kind and put me back on the meds and I would eat. I told her I hurt too bad to get out of bed to get my food or use the restroom. I told her I knew in her heart she took her job because she wanted to help people. She said she didn't know why the other Dr. discontinued the meds, due to the fact that I'm in chronic care and have Hep-C. She said the x-ray showed a fracture of my shoulder that will never heal and will always give me problems. She said she was going to call her boss and explain my problem and said she would do so if I came off my hunger strike. She said if I had any more problems to please send her a request. And the next day my meds started coming to me three times a day.

Five days was really rough and I think it was on my fourth day I actually ate a soup dry, then made myself throw it back up just to get rid of the thought of food. Everybody told me I was stupid and doing it for nothing and it wasn't going to work, but I let all that go and put my headphones on and listened to the forest on my mp4 player and read my books. It's crazy because a few hours ago a Sgt. that's cool with me said, "I give you props Cody. You stood up and didn't give in and stuck to your plan." I said, "No, Sgt., you got it wrong. I stood up for what was not right—them taking not only my pills, but my friend's and beings that actually need the shit."

It's wrong for a Dr. to sit behind a desk and not even examine a prisoner and say they are okay and take them off a med they have been on for years. It really just pisses me the f– off. They can't do Roy like that. That's a med they took him off cold turkey and withdrawals could really hurt him. Bro, I really hope he is okay and can find a way through this. Hang in there Roy, Bro. I got love for you Bro.

Hard News

John's letters were as thoughtful as ever, always taking a more cerebral perspective on Buddhist teachings and practice, while also describing the daily goings-on in prison. He also sometimes wrote about his life before prison, including his unhappy last marriage ("My wife and I hated each other. Fought all the time. Two people from different worlds"). But he was shaken to the core when he received a letter from her in 2016 telling him that their son had been dead for the past six years, killed in a shooting.

The news renewed his determination to arrange a visit with his daughter, now 12, who had been devastated when she last attempted to visit him several years earlier and was unable to see him because he was in the Hole. In anticipation of her visit, John had been working hard to qualify for "good time" in prison, a status that would allow him better visitation opportunities, including contact visitation. But a run-in with a female guard caused a setback. The guard accused him of masturbating in front of her during an inspection. John disputes the claim—he says another prisoner paid her to get him in trouble—and several prisoners who witnessed the incident testified in

John's support that nothing inappropriate occurred. Nevertheless, John was disciplined, sent to the Hole, and stripped of the "good time" he was counting on for a visit with his daughter.

John

I wrote my wife and daughter and explained what happened. I let them know I was filing my grievance procedures (which can take up to 6 months) and to just have patience.

The last letter I got in 2010 was from my daughter, who told me that if I didn't love her enough after all these years, to not bother writing again. I sent 5 huge packages of everything I had accumulated for her over the years. I wrote her and told her I'm sorry you feel that way, especially when I am innocent.

I dropped the suit I had on my grievance procedures and haven't heard from them since. That's the full story. For about a week after I got my daughter's letter, I was planning to put the officer into a coma. Then I let it go. What would it have accomplished? Nothing. I wouldn't undo what was done.

· · · · · · · ·

Just got off behavior control. What they do is put you in solitary confinement with your boxer shorts and one blanket with the blowers on full. That's all you get. Nothing else. No Beanie. No shirt. No socks. No shoes. Nothing. No soap. No toothpaste. No cups. Nothing for 72 hours. I bundled up in a ball under the side of the concrete table wall to let the air flow over the top of me. My wolf is gone. I couldn't even make myself pissed off. I nonchalantly told them, do what you gotta do. Wasn't mad when they shot me [with pepper spray] in the nuts or the eyes. It was my actions that caused it. How can I be mad at them? No matter where they may put me, no matter what they may do to me, no matter where I may be in the world, they cannot stop my thinking. They cannot control my heart, nor oppress my soul. To them, all they have is a physical shell.

A New Life

On January 25, 2017, Tad was released from prison after 15 years. Although his grandmother had passed away, he made arrangements to live with his sister while he got back on his feet, and traveled to Nacogdoches, Texas, to move in with her.

Tad

Regaining my freedom has left me seeing "freedom," in a whole different light. The way information flys at me out here feels smothering, and at times overwhelming. Fear was gripping me about six months before my release, fear that I would fail in my attempts to re-enter society. That all those years, in there practicing, educating myself, trying to stay focused, would all get shattered, instantly!

I knew what type of family I have! But, now that I am able to see them face to face, my heart only bleeds more sympathy for them. They are bitter, mean individuals. The element of kindness is nowhere to be found in most of them.

When I went to visit my mom & stepdad to pick up some of my artwork & property, as soon as I walked in their apartment, my heart hit the floor. The way they lived was devastating, such filth filled their place. My mother looked so pain-strickened, it was sad. She asked me if I still loved her. Yes, was my answer. But how she was living was sickening.

My stepdad looked like the walking dead! A man I once had so much hatred for, on the day I saw him and my mom for the first time in over 15 years, I told him to come give me a hug. And while hugging him, I told him I forgave him. No more hate inside for that man. I even told him I loved him. That was something I never thought I would do. BUT, I did it! All that practice in [prison] paid off. Years of hatred within myself turned to complete understanding of need, compassion & kindness.

· · · · · · · ·

Doing all my best is all I can do from this moment on, since my release. A part of me feels that now that I've obtained the knowledge of how to practice a life of mindfulness, compassion, kindness, etc., I feel that I am obligated to stand courageous, and let my character shine. Shine as an example. Hopefully, some of my family members will see!!

Will I try to force them to change, or else? No. But what is the "else"? The else was me not even coming to Texas when I got released. Not even giving them a chance. I asked my sister, would she have been mad at me if I was to have went straight to another state, and not came here? She told me, "I'd have never forgave you." Her heart would have been crushed.

I've done explained to the family, I want to be more involved in their lives, [but] if I see things going a wrong direction, I'm leaving! But, if I see where my light is creating guidance, then shouldn't it be my duty & honor to stand for them? My practice is my new life!

My practice is and will be continued. Even after my release. Around my nieces, I use a lot of words like kindness, mindfulness, compassion, sacrifice, dedication, discipline. I got into a long discussion the other night about the benefits of meditation.

Tomorrow I plan on going on-line to see if I can't find some local Buddhist groups in my area. See if I wouldn't maybe become a regular member to one or two.

I've mainly been really focused on my artwork. Getting it on-line to start networking and producing. Once all the kinks are worked out, I will start sharing artwork with these local Buddhist groups. Donate a little art maybe to them.

While in prison, there were some times I felt I would not make it out of there alive. But I find myself now with so many mixed emotions. Some I never got to truly understand—nor enjoy.

"Simply Existing"

In 2016, Roy's health began deteriorating due to his hepatitis and the rheumatoid arthritis causing the deformity of his hands. His pain became increasingly severe. Meditation and reflection on his Buddhist practice helped him cope with the pain, anger, and depression.

Roy

Everyone has a "breaking point" regarding how much pain/torture they can endure before they lose to anger/hate. I'm not living, simply existing. Even in prison one needs at least a small amount of quality of life. I'm afraid if I don't take action soon I will lose my heart to anger. I can only take so much pain. I'm gonna read my Dhammapada, then go. I come from emptiness and return to emptiness. You'll recognize me when ya ain't lookin' for me. You'll see a peaceful freedom and contentment.

. . . .

Hey Bro it's been a rough f–in' night. Finally got the guards to take me to the infirmary to get a shot of anything to get the pain to ease just a little. The nurse on duty is very kind and compassionate even though so many of these guys disrespect her. She tried to convince the Dr. on call to authorize a shot when she finally got him on the phone. The Dr. told her I'd be ok and to give me some ibuprofen and an ice pack. When she got off the phone, she gave me the pain shot anyway and said she was quitting soon as her shift was over. She said her brother was a medic in the army who treated the jihadists with more humanity than she was seeing here.

. . . .

My heels hurt so bad that I can't stand it. I can't stand. I begged them to cut off my feet. I said I would sign any waiver they want. Today they took away my last prescription for pain—ibuprofen. How can they be so cruel? They told me I could buy ibuprofen at the commissary.

. . . .

Sometimes I do get angry but become aware of it pretty fast because my breathing is so deeply, intensely affected and my pulse becomes so erratic and out of sync. Our bodies tell us our mind has gotten out of control, out of focus. By tensing up I cause myself more pain. Pain is one hell of a Teacher.

. . . .

Came to sit on my bed but saw a tiny tree frog stuck on my window. It wasn't a clever source of electronic surveillance. I got closer and closer while moving my mattress in place so I could "sit" with "Dogen" (that's what I named him) as being part of his sangha. I watched him just "BE," just breathe and be, being in the moment. Moment by moment. All the anger in me was slowly released with every beat of Dogen's heart. I just couldn't fathom how much pain and suffering I was causing myself. I realized I could "Let Go" of my anger and that in turn would lessen my self-inflicted pain and suffering. It's like flippin' a light switch. The anger had me seeking darkness, a dark path, but the flip side: going into the Sweat Lodge where I do visualizations, watching and feeling anger as it sweats outta me, realizing the ugly intentions influenced by anger. I was feeling my body react in a positive way, a relaxed looseness. Anger is not only a stupid waste of time and energy, it causes pain and suffering; everything about it is negative.

. . . .

As for what's going on in my mind when I meditate, for quite some time now I've been totally focused on visualizations for my liver and kidneys and insides/spine-backbone as a whole. When I do regular sitting meditation I ease into a smooth inhale/exhale, a natural flow, then I start counting to 12, counting and breathing, then I kind of see space in a "Blue Luminescence" that seems infinite. Let shit go and not just see that infinite Blue, but merge and become the infinite Blue. I don't take my f– ups into my meditation. I realize pretty quick when I get angry and turn anger into Compassionate Loving kindness. I use my empty space meditation to kind of get centered. As I leave my meditation I visualize the Blue Luminescence turn to Loving kindness.

· · · · · · · ·

I don't think I've got three years left but suspect it is closer to two. It isn't just me that has come to this conclusion. A nurse I've known for 10 years was changing my IV port to my left arm because antibiotics are very hard on the veins and she said, "Roy, you've had hepatitis since 1994 and I'm sure you kept shooting heroin and anything else you could find for another 10 years. Am I right?"

I said, "Right on target plus drinking some form of booze for as long as I was conscious."

She sighed and said, "Roy, I've been nursing since 1974," and then I cut her off saying, "I got maybe two or three years left then it'll be over."

She asked me, "How the hell did you figure that out?" I told her I could just feel it. I said it felt like my life force was slowly losing its power, like a dimmer switch slowing fading to blackness.

She looked at me and she had tears in her eyes. Bro, told her "Nuttin' 2it," smiled and said, "you know I'm Buddhist and will rebirth as an Eagle and fly free and happy." She smiled, then said, "If it's at all possible, you probably will."

EPILOGUE

I'm in a state of "chaos" within. I originally came to prison having to serve five years before I would be eligible for parole in 2012. I was three months from the parole board and having medical issues after a surgery. I chose to take a nurse hostage in the infirmary in order to get a transfer to a unit to get medical help. I'd seen two other prisoners previously do it, their motive was to get pills, mine got me a kidnapping charge. I went to trial and received forty-two years. Since that day I have had no peace within, all my hopes, dreams, and aspirations have vanished! A little over a month after my trial I escaped my cell at the supermax, coming out on a tier and beating and stabbing an officer. I've made attempts here at this unit and was again recently successful in breaking out and stabbing another officer. It's as if I'm at a constant war with the suits and with myself.

I'd first spoke with Tad Price, a man I've done time around for many years and was always amazed at his peaceful state even amongst the confusion that surrounds us here! I as well know John Bruno who radiates a sense of certainty, peacefulness, and calmness. They both credit this peacefulness to Buddism and the Buddist teachings! I seek and need this in my life. I'm respectfully requesting you teach me about Buddism. I will be a diligent student grateful of your time and energy. That is if you would be kind enough to teach me!

I received this letter from inmate Christopher Brewer, who went by the moniker Twisted, just as I was finishing work on this book. As so often happens when I write to prisoners, I was amazed by his story, his pain, and his resilience.

When I began writing to Roy Tester in 2009, I had no idea that it was the start of not just one, but many relationships that would change my life. As Roy introduced me to John and Tad, then Cody, my circle of new partners expanded, but it didn't end there.

Over the subsequent years, our partnership has continued to grow. Roy is still alive and continues to touch lives and help others, introducing more prisoners to Buddhism, kindness, and meditation, even though his health and disability makes it difficult for him to leave his cell. And John, Tad, and

Cody, by extending kindness to others and living the values and principles of Buddhism, have brought still more partners into the group. As time went on, I began to hear from many of the men who were reached by this practice. All in all, I have exchanged letters on and off with more than a dozen inmates at Tucker Max, including Chris, Mike, Bradley, Steven, Robert (aka "Nuub"), Neil , and now Christopher.

There has been no greater validation of my work with Roy than to see the seeds of kindness and mindfulness we planted together begin to grow and take on a life of their own, touching the lives of more and more men in one of the most notorious prisons in the country. Separately, I began a correspondence with Ernesto Rodriguez, an inmate at Pelican Bay State Prison in California, and worked with him as he designed a "pay it forward" project that would prepare other prisoners for release.

Although my wife and I had been active with social justice issues in the 1960s, particularly in the area of education, I had no experience with the criminal justice system, and had never before worked with prisoners. Gaining such sudden access to their most private thoughts and the intimate details of their lives came as a shock. But it also opened my eyes to their deep humanity and impressed upon me the profound potential of every human being to make a difference in the world. Undeniably, each of these men has done terrible things, and yet, remarkably, they were able to change not only their own lives, but the lives of others.

Cody continues to suffer from severe pain. An MRI eventually showed he had a herniated disk. He was moved to a handicap-accessible cell and went through several surgeries to fix the problem, without success. Barely 31, with debilitating pain and now wearing a colostomy bag, he is coming to terms with spending perhaps another 50 years in prison. At times, he has shared suicidal thoughts. And yet he has also shared how he has been able to find a sense of peace and purpose in his calling to Buddhism and in Buddhist teachings on the nature of suffering and impermanence. Go to my blog (http://feedkindness.com/blog/) to see how Cody deals with his fourth back surgery that has left him in a wheelchair for the rest of his life.

Tad is adjusting to his new life outside of prison. Within a few weeks of his release he had found a job and was looking for a second, part-time job to help him get back on his feet. When he wrote to me about his plans, he said that a top goal was to find and become involved with local Buddhist groups, and to develop a network to begin selling his paintings. Although he will face many challenges in the years to come, Tad says he is committed to continuing his practice, maintaining his connection with the dharma, and taking each day as it comes. Go to my blog (http://feedkindness.com/blog/) to see how Tad continues his practice after taking the fall for his brother, to prevent the police from revoking his brother's parole because of drug-possession.

John still writes to me about deep loneliness. A few years ago, he wrote a song about his regrets, and I recorded it. At his request, I sent a copy of the recording to his family. After his daughter listened to it, she wrote to him again. It's not yet clear if she will agree to a visit in the future.

Roy has gone through ups and downs, both mentally and physically. By late 2015, his disability had progressed to the point that he could no longer hold a pen. Although that put an end to our letter-writing, we have been able to maintain our friendship and practice through regular phone calls, talking about once a month. In a recent conversation, he described how he was coming to terms with his pain. Far from giving up, he said he had found strength in facing it "like a samurai." In early 2017, a new policy at the prison allowed inmates in Roy's barracks to leave their cells in shifts for two hours at a time. The change meant that Roy was able to move around freely and interact one-on-one with other prisoners for the first time in years. I heard a renewed energy in his voice as he described how he was able to spend a little time talking to his neighbors each day and spread kindness. "If I can get you for five or 10 minutes first thing in the morning," he said, "I'm going to get you feeling positive before you leave my porch."

As for me, writing to prisoners eventually became almost a part-time job. I found myself spending five to six hours a week either responding to their letters or making telephone calls on their behalf. It was around this time that I knew I had to document the experience in a book. Beyond my duty to engage with these men as a lay minister, I realized that the stories they were telling me—stories of suffering, redemption, and ultimately trans-formation—needed to be shared.

Working on this book, I was reminded again of the profound power of kindness. It reinforced in me the importance of acting with kindness in my own life, inspired in me a new sense of gratitude, and gave me a broader perspective on my own disappointments. Now, when worry or pain keep me awake at night, I recite their names silently to myself, like a prayer: Cody, Tad, John, Roy. Thinking of them reminds me of what life can be.

GLOSSARY

Attachment The desire for things to be a certain way; clinging or craving; in Buddhism, considered to be one of the roots of suffering.

Bodhisattva A highly advanced practitioner of Buddhism, one who attains enlightenment in a spirit of compassion for others.

Buddha The founder of Buddhism, also called Siddhartha, Gautama Buddha, or Shakyamuni Buddha; any practitioner of Buddhism who has attained full awakening or enlightenment.

Buddha nature This is the fundamental nature that we all share, the inherent human instinct toward the good, towards kindness.

Dalai Lama The spiritual leader of Tibetan Buddhism, known for his wisdom and compassion.

Dharma The core teachings of Buddhism. Dharma also means the law or the way things are.

Dhammapada A classic Buddhist scripture containing teachings of the Buddha.

Four Noble Truths A core Buddhist teaching: First, that suffering exists; second, that the root of suffering is attachment; third, that only the end of attachment will end suffering; fourth, that freedom can be attained by following the Noble Eightfold Path.

Full Lotus A sitting posture for meditation, in which the right foot rests on the left thigh and the left foot on the right thigh.

Gassho A hand gesture in which the palms are pressed together with fingertips pointing up, often used in greeting, or to express gratitude and humility.

Karma Literally translated as "action," the Buddhist principle of cause and effect.

Koan A riddle, paradox, tiny story or question used to train the mind, especially in Zen Buddhism. In some schools of Zen, students contemplate koans as a practice.

Loving-Kindness The sense of love and well-wishing toward all living things.

Mala beads Buddhist prayer beads used for counting while reciting or chanting a mantra (aloud or silently).

Mantra A word or short verse of scripture that may be recited as a focus in meditation.

Metta Sutta A classic Buddhist scripture on the theme of loving-kindness and goodwill.

Meditation A family of practices aimed at disciplining, focusing, and calming the mind.

Merit In Buddhism, the power or positive energy that accrues as a result of meditation, good works or positive thoughts. Merit can be transferred to others.

Mindfulness Mindfulness is awareness that arises through paying attention, on purpose, in the present moment, non-judgmentally. The practice of mindfulness often arouses feelings of calmness and peace.

Mudra A pose or gesture, usually of the hands, used in certain Buddhist rituals or meditation. Each mudra has its own meaning, such as "fear not," "touching the earth," or "welcome."

Noble Eightfold Path The eight practices at the core of Buddhism, forming the path to transcend suffering and attain enlightenment. These practices include right understanding, right thought, right speech, right action, right livelihood, right effort, right mindfulness, and right concentration.

Practice In Buddhism, daily activities like meditation, as well as personal commitments like following Buddhist teachings and precepts. Through practice, a student of Buddhism trains the mind and heart.

Precepts Buddhism's code of ethics, including refraining from killing, stealing, sensual indulgence, harmful speech, intoxication, and other guidelines.

Rakusu A symbolic, bib-like garment worn by Zen priests and some students of Zen.

Samsara The cycle of life and death in the material world.

Sangha A Community of Buddhist practitioners.

Sit A term used informally by Buddhists to refer to the act of meditating.

Skillful means Wise ways of speaking and acting.

Vesak the most important Buddhist festival, commemorating the birth, enlightenment, and death of the Buddha,

Walking meditation A practice of calming the mind and cultivating awareness through slow, mindful walking.

BIBLIOGRAPHY

Baraz, James, and Shoshana Alexander. *Awakening Joy: 10 Steps to Happiness.* Berkeley: Parallax Press, 2012.

Chödrön, Pema. *When Things Fall Apart: Heart Advice for Difficult Times.* Boulder: Shambhala Publications, 2000.

Hanh, Thich Nhat. *The Heart of Buddha's Teaching: Transforming Suffering into Peace, Joy, and Liberation.* Berkeley: Parallax Press, 1998.

Brasington, Leigh. "18 Translations of the Metta Sutta—Sutta Nipata I.8." Web. June 9, 2015. http://www.leighb.com/mettasuttas.htm

His Holiness the Dalai Lama. *Ethics for the New Millennium.* Boston: Little, Brown and Co., 1999.

"Prison Ashram Project." *The Human Kindness Foundation.* Web. 2014.

Jiyu-Kennett, P.T.N.H. *Zen is Eternal Life.* Mount Shasta: Shasta Abbey Press, 1999.

McCasland, David. "The Challenge of Confinement." *Our Daily Bread,* Dec. 27, 2013. Web. http://odb.org/2013/12/27/the-challenge-of-confinement/

McGuinnes, Keith. "Sewing a Rakusu." *Sitting Quietly, Doing Nothing,* Oct. 15, 2012. Web. https://mcguinnes.wordpress.com/2012/10/15/sewing-a-rakus

Tuttiett, Mokyugo Adrian. "What-the-Sutra-Says: The Sandokai." *International Zen Association United Kingdom.* Dec. 28, 2012. Web. http://www.izauk.org/multimedia-archive/what-the-sutra-says-the-sandokai/

Young, William P. *The Shack.* Newbury Park: Windblown Media, 2008.

BIBLIOGRAPHY

RESOURCES

Kindness Ideas

Feed Kindness Starve Harm:
Practicing Mindful Kindness in Personal Situations
http://feedkindness.com/resources/

This Resources for Mindful Living link provides examples, activities, and research findings for using mindfulness to clearly see and change unkind habits while cultivating kind habits in a variety of personal situations: self care, couples, friends, parents, and co-workers.

Greater Good Science Center
http://greatergood.berkeley.edu/resources#none

This site provides links to organizations that "promote social and emotional well-being through research, practice, or both." Categories of organizations include:

Altruism & Heroism   Gratitude
Anti-Racism & Tolerance   Happiness
Empathy   Mind & Body
Family & Couples   Mindfulness
Forgiveness   Work & Career

Making Mindful Kindness Part of Community Participation
http://feedkindness.com/resources/mindful-community-participation/

This Feed Kindness Starve Harm link provides examples, activities, research, and resources for how to practice mindful kindness while serving your community.

Working toward Social Justice Using Mindful Kindness
http://feedkindness.com/mindful-social-justice/

This Feed Kindness Starve Harm link provides examples, activities, research, and resources for how to practice mindful kindness while working toward social justice.

KindSpring
http://www.kindspring.org/ideas/

KindSpring provides kindness ideas across different themes, including For Friends and Family, For Yourself, and For the Elderly.

Random Acts of Kindness Foundation
https://www.randomactsofkindness.org/kindness-ideas

Random Acts believes in spreading kindness throughout schools, communities, and homes. They provide ideas in many categories including ideas you can do for strangers, ideas just for you, ideas you can do at work, ideas to show kindness to your neighbors, and ideas for your community.

Buddhism and Prisons

Compassion Works for All
http://www.compassionworksforall.org

The mission of Compassion Works for All is "to offer healing and hope by living and teaching compassion, especially to the disenfranchised and people in prison."

Engaged Buddhism Resources from DharmaNet International
http://www.dharmanet.org/lcengaged.htm

This organization provides information about engaged Buddhism in many aspects of society, not just prisons.

National Buddhist Prison Sangha
https://zmm.mro.org/national-buddhist-prison-sangha/

The National Buddhist Prison Sangha is a nationwide network of Buddhist volunteers. Their mission is "to sustain a correspondence program in Zen Buddhist practice with inmates across the country in prison facility settings."

Prison Mindfulness Institute
http://prisonmindfulness.org

The mission of the institute is "to provide prisoners, prison staff, and prison volunteers with the most effective, evidence-based tools for rehabilitation, self-transformation, and personal & professional development. In particular, we provide and promote the use of proven effective mindfulness-based interventions (MBIs)."

The Author's Buddhist Practice

Order of Buddhist Contemplatives
obcon.org

The Order of Buddhist Contemplatives (OBC) is "an international monastic order of men and women who, together with lay ministers of the Order and our congregations and affiliated meditation groups, are dedicated to practicing the Serene Reflection Meditation tradition of Buddhism, also called Soto Zen."

Shasta Abbey Buddhist Monastery
shastaabbey.org

Shasta Abbey, located near Mount Shasta in Northern California, is a "Buddhist monastery in the Serene Reflection Meditation (Soto Zen) Tradition. A monastery of the Order of Buddhist Contemplatives, it was founded by Rev. Master Jiyu-Kennett in 1970 as a training place for Buddhist monastics and a place of practice for lay people. We offer the Dharma to all who wish to come." The Abbey offers retreats, ceremonies, teaching, and spiritual counseling.

Throssel Hole Buddhist Abbey
http://throssel.org.uk

Throssel Hole Buddhist Abbey, located in Northern England, is a "monastery and retreat centre devoted to the practice of meditation within the Serene Reflection Meditation Tradition of Buddhism (Soto Zen). The monastic community offers retreats, festivals and other events for anyone who wishes to learn about or deepen their practice of meditation, and to explore more fully its fundamental relevance in our daily lives."

Prisons and Prison Reform

The Real Cost of Prisons Project
http://www.realcostofprisons.org

This project "brings together justice activists, artists, researchers and women and men directly experiencing the impact of mass criminalization who are working to end the carceral state." The site includes writing, comics, and music created by prisoners.

Yes! Magazine
http://www.yesmagazine.org/peace-justice/beyond-prisons

The Peace & Justice section of Yes! magazine provides articles about improving, reforming, and abolishing prisons.

Increasing Compassion

A Fearless Heart: How the Courage to Be Compassionate Can Transform Our Lives, by Thupten Jinpa (Penguin, 2015). Part 2 is particularly helpful.

Lovingkindness: The Revolutionary Art of Happiness, by Sharon Salzberg and Jon Kabat-Zinn (Shambhala, 2002).

Inspirational Movies

Inspirational movies based on true stories
http://www.imdb.com/list/ls0539264b82/

The author of this list recommends 90 inspirational movies including The Great Debaters, The Vernon Johns Story, McFarland USA, Invictus, A Civil Action, and Selma.

IMDb: Movies Tagged "Inspirational"
http://www.imdb.com/lists/tag/Inspirational/

This link provides users' lists of recommended inspirational movies.

ABOUT THE AUTHOR

Doug Carnine is a lay minister in the Order of Buddhist Contemplatives and a founding member of the Eugene Buddhist Priory. A practicing Buddhist for more than 40 years, his first teacher and lay ordination master was Rev. Master Houn Jiyu-Kennett, who was herself ordained into the Chinese Buddhist Sangha in Malaysia by the Very Reverend Seck Kim Seng, Archbishop of Malacca. Then in Japan in 1963, the Very Reverend Keido Chisan Koho Zenji, Chief Abbot of Dai Hon Zan Soji-ji, one of the two chief training monasteries of Soto Zen, transmitted her and later certified her as Roshi (Zen Master). Carnine was ordained as a lay Buddhist in 1975. He is also a longtime practitioner of Tai Chi.

An award-winning professor of Education at the University of Oregon for almost 40 years, Carnine received a presidential appointment to serve on the board of the National Institute for Literacy. He is also the author of more than 100 scholarly publications, six books, and numerous textbooks on subjects ranging from math and science to world history and English composition.

Since his retirement from the university in 2010, Carnine has focused on the study and practice of mindful kindness. His work inspired him to write the book *How Love Wins: The Power of Mindful Kindness,* and to create the website feedkindness.com.

Carnine and his wife, Linda, also a lay Buddhist minister, have two daughters.

CPSIA information can be obtained
at www.ICGtesting.com
Printed in the USA
FSHW021301170119
55090FS